ENVIRONMENTAL SCIENCE
MULTIDISCIPLINARY COURSE
for
B.A/ B.SC/ B.COM/ 1st Semester

REFERENCE BOOK
Prepared as Per FYUGP Syllabus

Nagaland University

NOHOCHEM SANGTAM

Copyright © 2024-Nohochem Sangtam

All Rights Reserved.

ISBN:979-8894987439 (Paperback)
ISBN: 979-8894987446(Hardcase)
First Published 2024

Made with ❤ on the Notion Press Platform

www.notionpress.com

Published by: Notion Press
Notion Press Media Private Limited's
Email:editor@notionpress.com and its registered
Address is No.50, Chettiyar
Agaram Main Road Vanagaram Chennai TN 600092 IN

Preface

This book is published with the intention of helping students preparing for Environmental Science. The book has been prepared in a very basic information on the prescribed syllabus. The Book will be helpful for any examination that contains the syllabus of Environment, Natural resources, Biodiversity and its conservation, environmental pollution, waste management and disaster management.

The book consists of four Unit which is required by the Multidisciplinary Course (MDC)first semester under FYUGP - Nagaland University.

Lastly, I feel great pleasure in expressing my deep sense of gratitude to Notion Press publishing house, for publication of this book.

As a writer, it is my constant and sincere effort to improve this book is there are any shortcomings, mistake, or errors in it, I heartily apologise for that. Any suggestion for the improvement of this book will be most welcome.

Nohochem Sangtam

Date:01/1/2024

MULTIDISCIPLINARY COURSE: ENVIRONMENTAL SCIENCE
SULLYBUS -B.A/BSC/B.COM 1ST SEMESTER

Unit1: Ecosystem and the Environment

Definition, Scope and importance of Environmental science; Concept, Structure, and functions of an Ecosystem; Bio-geographical classification of India; Value of biodiversity;Need for Public

awareness towards conservation.

Unit 2: Natural Resources

Renewable and non-renewable resources; Use and over exploitation of natural resources; Role of individual in conservation of natural resources.

Population growth; Impact of human population growth on natural resources and environment;

Sustainable development.

Unit 3: Environmental Pollution, Laws &Management

a. Definition, Causes, Effects and Control/Preventive measures of Air, Water, Soil and Noise

pollution.

b. Legal, administrative and constitutional provisions for environmental protection in India;

Evolution and development of International Environmental laws and treaties; Concept and

scope of environmental Management; Solid waste management; Waste-to-wealth technologies.

Unit 4: Environmental hazards

Definition - Hazard, vulnerability, and risk;

Strategies for mitigation - warning system, forecasting, emergency preparedness;

Education and Training Activities,

planning for Rescue and Relief works.

CONTENTS	Page

UNIT ONE
ECOSYSTEM AND THE ENVIRONMENTAL SCIENCE

1.1.Environmental Science

Environmental science is the systematic study of our environment and our place in it. Environmental science is highly interdisciplinary. It integrates information from biology, chemistry, geography, agriculture and many other fields.

Environment study deals with the analysis of the processes in water, air, land, soil and organisms which leads to pollute environment.

1.2. Scope of Environmental Science

i. Increase public awareness

ii. Provides knowledge of environmental issues

iii. Sensitizes individuals about the necessity of sustainable

iv. Development

v. Sensitization of students/schools as well as college on various environmental issues.

vi. Creating environment awareness among masses

vii. Engagement of target groups in environment friendly action and thereby inculcation of proper attitude towards the environment and its conservation through community interaction.

According to UNESCO (1971), the objectives of environmental science are:

i. Creating the awareness about environmental problems among people.

ii. Imparting basic knowledge about the environment and its allied problems.

iii. Developing an attitude of concern for the environment

    iv. Motivating public to participate in environment protection and environment improvement.

    v. Acquiring skills to help the concerned individuals in identifying and solving environmental problems.

    vi. Striving to attain harmony with nature

1.3 Importance of Environmental Science

The importance of environmental science is describing as follows:

    i. Clarification of modern environmental concept like how to conserve biodiversity.

    ii. Helping people know the more sustainable way of living

    iii. Making masses understand how to use the natural resource in a efficient way.

    iv. Developing awareness about the behavior of organism under natural conditions.

    v. Creating knowledge about the inter-relationship between organisms in populations and communities.

    vi. Creating awareness and educating people regarding environmental issues and problems at local, national and internationals level.

1.4. Concept of Ecosystem

The term ecosystem was proposed by a **British Ecologist A.G Tansley in 1935-** its "Eco" part means environment and the "System" part implies a complex of coordinated units.

Ecosystem defined as the basic fundamental, structural and functional unit of ecology which comprises of the biotic community and abiotic environment.

Ecosystem is the functional unit of nature where living organisms interact with each other and with their environment. Ecosystem includes plants, trees, animals, fish, birds, microorganisms, water, soil, and people.

In general, the structure of an ecosystem has two major components as biotic and abiotic. These two classes of components interact with each other to create ecosystem.

1.5.Structure of Ecosystem

Biotic (Living)	Abiotic (Non-Living)
Biotic components includes the living organisms and are classified into Producer, Consumers and Decomposer. **1.Producer:** **Producers(Autotrophs-self nourishing).** Primary producers are basically green plants and certain bacteria and algae. They synthesize carbohydrates from inorganic raw materials like carbon-dioxide and water in the presence of sunlight by the process of photosynthesis from themselves, and supply indirectly to other non-producers. In terrestrial ecosystem, producers are basically herbaceous and woody plants while in aquatic ecosystem producers are various species of microscopic algae. $6CO_2 + 6H_2O \rightarrow C_6H_{12}O_6 + 6O_2$ **2. Consumers :(Phagotrophs)** Consumer cannot make their own food but are directly or indirectly dependent on producers for obtaining food. They depend on organic food derived from plants, animals or both.	**1. Abiotic Components** Abiotic components are the nonliving components parts of the world. **i. Light/Energy:** Energy from the sun is essential for maintenance of life. In the case of plants, the sun directly supplies the necessary energy. Since animals cannot use solar energy directly they obtain it indirectly by eating plants or animals or both. Energy determines the distribution of organisms in the environment. **ii.Rainfall:** Water is essential for all living beings. Majority of bio-chemical reactions takes place in an aqueous medium. Water helps to regulate body temperature.

They feed on plants or animals or both. On the basis of their food sources.

Primary Consumer (Herbivores) are which feed mainly on Plants. Example, Cow, Rabbit,deer,goat,grass hopper etc.
Secondary Consumers/
Primary Carnivores:
They feed herbivores.Example snakes, cats, fox, frogs, birds etc.

Tertiary Consumers/
Secondary Carnivores:
They are large carnivores which eat the flesh of the secondary consumers Example:
Wolves, peacock, owl, fishes etc.
Top Carnivores: These are the largest carnivores, which eat the flesh of the tertiary consumers and can't be eaten up by any other animal's
For example: Lion, Tiger and vulture.
Omnivores-Consume both plants and animals. Example Man, Monkey
3. Decomposers(Reducers)
They are also called **saprotrophs.**
They are microorganism, bacteria and fungi which obtain energy and nutrients by decomposing dead organic substances(detritus) of plants and animals origin.
The products of decomposition such as inorganic nutrients which are released in the ecosystem and revised by producers and thus recycled.

Further, water bodies from the habitat for many aquatic plants and animals.

iii. wind: It controls the formation of clouds, fog, dew etc.

iv.Temperature:
Temperature is a critical factor of the environment which greatly influences survival of organisms. Organisms can tolerate only a certain range of temperature and humidity.
v. Atmosphere
The earth's atmosphere is responsible for creating conditions suitable for the existence of a healthy biosphere on this planet.
vi.Substratum
Land is covered by soil and a wide variety of microbes, protozoa, fungi and small animals (invertebrates) strive in it.Roots of plants pierce through the soil to absorb water and nutrients. Organisms can be terrestrial or aquatic. Terrestrial animals live on land. Aquatic plants, animals and microbes

Earthworm and certain soil organisms (such as nematods, and certain arthropods) are detritus feeders and help in the decomposition of organic matter and are called detritores	live in fresh water as well as in the salt water. Some microbes live even in hot water under the sea. **vii.Materials** **Organic components:** Protein, Carbohydrates, lipids and amino acid. **Inorganic components:** Carbon-dioxide, water, Nitrogen, phosphorus, sulphur and other ions and various metals that are essential for organisms to survive. **viii.Soil:** It determines the vegetation growth and pattern, under-ground flora and fauna through its constitution, origin, temperature range minerals etc.

1.6. Function of ecosystem

The functioning of an ecosystem refers to the ecosystem's analysis in terms of followings;

1.Physical(energy flow/Energy circuits)

2.Biological(Food chains,food web,

3.Ecological succession or Ecosystem Development

4.Biogeochemical(nutrients cycling) processes

6.1. Physical(energy flow/Energy circuits)

Flow of energy in ecosystem

The energy of sunlight is fixed in food production by green plants is passed through the ecosystem by food chains and food webs from one trophic level to another trophic level. In this way energy flows through the ecosystem.

The flow of energy from producer to the top consumers is called energy flow and is Unidirectional in Nature.

Flow of energy was proposed by **Lindemann in 1942** that the flow of energy occurs from one trophic level to the other at the rate of 10%.

During the process, a major portion(90%) on energy stored in food, is lost in the form of the heat energy. This heat is radiated into the atmosphere and cannot be reused by plants and animals.This energy flow is always unidirectional as the energy released from the sun can never be returned to the sun.

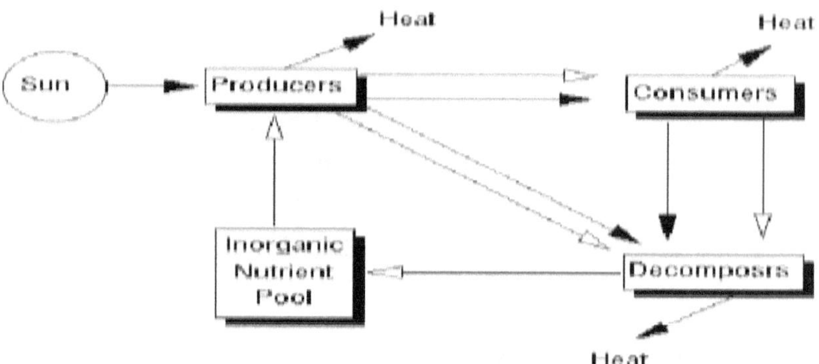

Fig 1.1 Flow of energy

Though, each plants or animals can be linked to several other plants or animals through several different linkages, these inter-linked chain can be depicted as a complex food web. This is, therefore, called the "web of life' that shows that there are thousands of interrelationships in nature. The energy in the ecosystem can be depicted in the form of a food pyramids or energy pyramidal or ecological pyramid.

6.2.Biological(Food Chains,food web).

Food chain:

The sequence of the eater's beings eaten producers transfer of food energy and it is known as Food chain. The biotic factors of the ecosystems are linked together by food. For example, the producers form the food for the herbivores, the herbivores for the food for the carnivores. The process of transfer of energy from producers to series of organisms to consumers is **called Food chain.** The position of organisms in the food chain or each step of the food chain is **referred as Trophic level.**

Types of food chain

Generally, food chains are classified in two types:

Grazing food chain and Decomposer/detritus food chain

i. Grazing Food Chain: Food chain begins with green plants and algae, and from there the energy passes through various levels of consumers. Human belongs to a grazer chain as well as either a primary or secondary consumer usually.

Example i.Grass→ Grass-hopper → Frog→ Snake →Owl

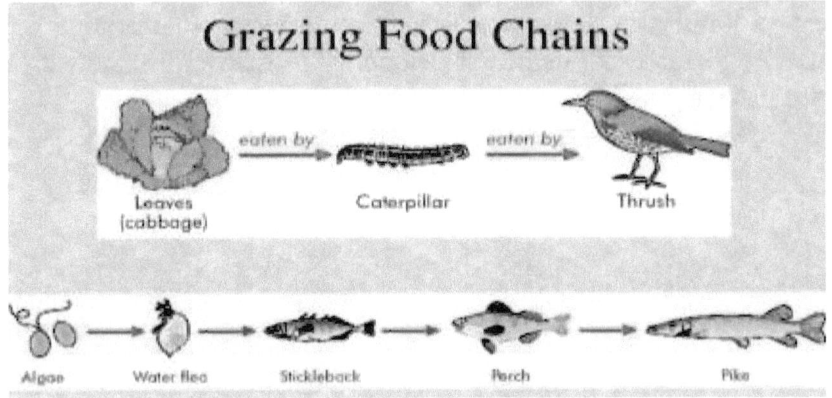

Fig.1.2 Grazing Food chain

2. Detritus/Decomposer food chain

Detritus food chains begin with dead organic matter called detritus; which mainly include fallen leaves, plants parts or dead animal bodies. These are consumed by insects, worms and bacteria etc.

These organism is responsible for decomposition of the waste and return of its nutrients to the environment for reuse by plants.

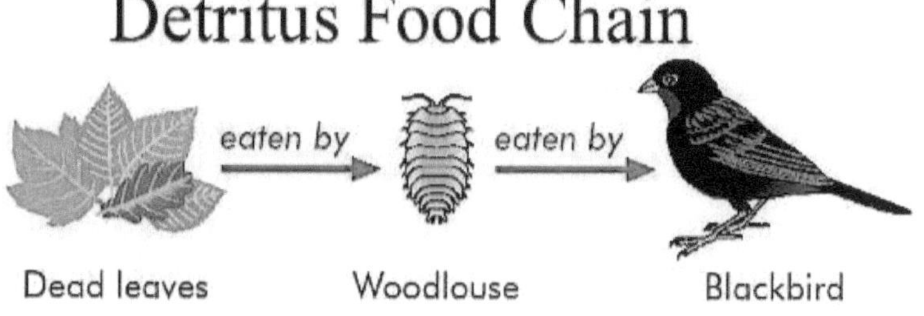

Fig:1.3 Decomposer Food chain

Food Web:

Food web is a network of food chains which become interconnected at various trophic levels so as to form a number of feeding connections amongst the different organisms of a biotic community.The various food chains in an ecosystems are interconnected or interlinked with each other to form a network **called Food web.** Food web is very important in maintaining the stability of an ecosystem. For example, the deleterious growth of grasses in a grassland is controlled by the herbivores.

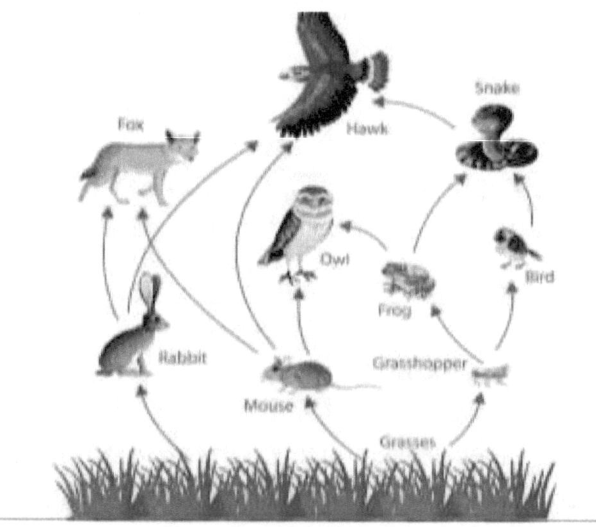

Fig.1.4 Food Web

6.3.Ecological succession or Ecosystem Development.

Ecological succession is the gradual and sequential replacement of one community by the other in an area over a period of time. According to E.P.Odum (1971), the ecological succession is an orderly process of community change in a unit area. It is the process of change in species composition in an ecosystem over time. In simpler terms, it is the process of Ecosystem Development in nature

1.Primary Succession

Starts from an area where there was no previous living matter. Example: rocks surface, newly created pond.
First community establishing the new area: Pioneer Community
Example: Lichens ,Phyto-planktons

Fig.1.5. Primary Succession

2.Secondary Succession:

Starts from a previously build-up substratum(already existing living matter
Sudden changes causes the disappearance of the existing community.Example: fire, snow fall, biotic interventions.Thus the area become devoid of any living matter. Secondary succession is comparatively rapid process.

Mechanism of Ecological Succession

Clements, being the most influential ecologists to suggest the mechanism of succession, in *Plant Succession: An Analysis of the Development of Vegetation* (1916), stated the succession a universal process of community development. He believed firmly that climate was the main driving factor in determining the type of vegetation during succession. As per his philosophy, climates are like genomes, and vegetation is like an organism whose characteristics its genome determines. The final step in vegetation succession he referred to as a climax. Another major point in Clements hypothesis is that the entire vegetation develops together as a single unit like an organism. This is known as the **super-organism theory.** He considered climax community to be a super-organism and succession the embryonic development of that organism. As an organism, climax arises, grows, matures and dies. The climax is capable of reproducing itself and every time a climax is produced, the essential steps are similar. Thus, succession is orderly, predictable and developmental process. It represents the holistic view.

He recognized the following basic processes in succession

1. Nudation:
It is the formation of a bare area without any life form. It may be a primary bare area if it is a new geological formation or a secondary bare area if formed due to destruction of existing vegetation. It may occur due to topographic factors (soil erosion, landslide, volcanic activity etc.), climatic factors (glacier, drought, frost, fire etc.) or biotic factors (deforestation, cultivation, insect outbreak, agricultural practices, overgrazing, etc.).

2. Invasion:
It is invasion and successive establishment of species in the bare area. It has three stages: **a) Migration:** In primary bare area, the seeds, spores or propagules of plants growing in adjacent areas arrive through dispersal by wind, water or animals. In secondary bare area, the propagules may already be present in the form of buried seeds or rootstocks - called as residuals. They are the pioneer stage of succession. **b) Ecesis** - It is the process of successful establishment of the species as a result of their adaptation to new area. The seeds and spores germinate, grow into adult forms and then reproduce. **c) Aggregation** - It is the final maturation of colonizing species; that is the growth of the population of each individual species. As the species reproduce, their number increases and population grow denser.

3. Competition and Co-action:

As the species number and size increase, it leads to competition for water, space and food. There can be inter-specific or intra-specific competition. The species which do not succeed in competition will disappear and the species which succeed will establish in that area. The species interact and affect each other's life in various ways called co-actions

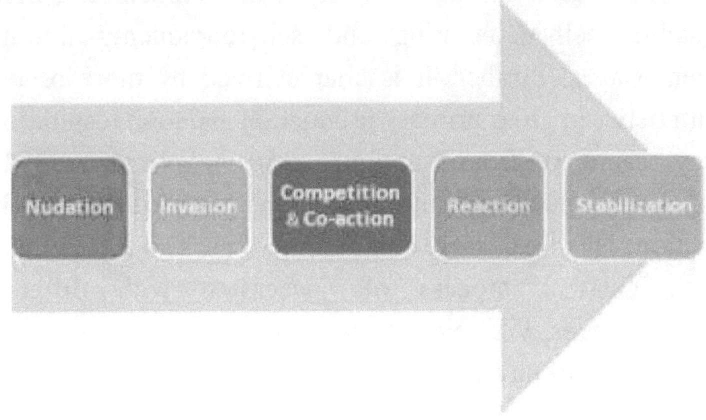

Fig. 1.6: Different processes of Ecological Succession

4. Reaction:

It is an important stage of succession and occurs between colonizing species and surrounding environment. The action of colonizing species changes the surrounding abiotic environment like soil, water, temperature and availability of nutrients. These changes make the place unfit for existing species and as a result they are replaced by a fit species.

For example, in a marshy area, reed swamp stage occur which includes amphibious plants with high evapo-transpiration rates. As a result, water availability in the area reduces and it will eventually become dry, thus becomes unsuitable for the existing plants. So, these autogenic changes by the plant species make them disappear and a new species which can grow in dry area will appear. This is termed

as reaction of surrounding environment. As a result, various communities form different seral stages. Each stage has its characteristic structure and species composition. A seral stage may last for 1 to 2 years or several decades.

5. Stabilization or Climax:

Eventually, a stage is reached when the final plant community becomes more or less stabilized for a longer period of time and maintains equilibrium with the surrounding environment. It is more mature, stable, self-maintaining and self-reproducing through development stages. Further, it is characterized by more or less equilibrium between gross primary production and total respiration, the energy captured from sunlight and energy released by decomposition, the uptake of nutrients and the return of nutrients by decomposition. This final stable community of the sere is the climax community. General process of succession with different developmental stages, viz., pioneer, seral and climax communities under the influence of physical environment, taking the examples of hydrosere and xerosere are shown in Fig below

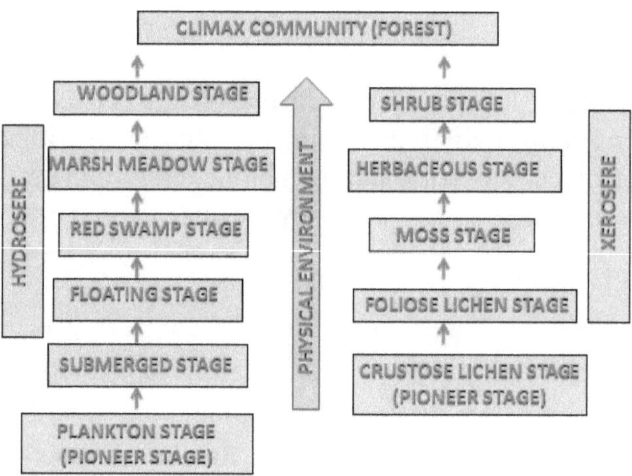

Fig:1.7: Diagram to show process of succession with pioneer, seral and climax communities under the influence of physical environment, taking the examples of hydrosere and xerosere

6.4.Biogeochemical(nutrients cycling) processes

The cycling of matter (carbon, hydrogen, nitrogen, oxygen, phosphorous. water, calcium, iron etc.) through an ecosystem is known as biogeochemical cycle.

Types of Biogeochemical Cycle

From the viewpoint of the ecosphere as a whole, biogeochemical cycle falls into two basic groups: A.Gaseous Cycle B. Sedimentary Cycle

A. Gaseous Cycle:

In gaseous nutrients cycle, the main reservoirs of chemical are the atmosphere and ocean

1 The carbon cycle, 2. The Nitrogen cycle 3. The Oxygen cycle

4. The Water Cycle (Hydrological Cycle)

B. Sedimentary Cycle:

In sedimentary cycle, the main reservoirs of chemical are rocks and soils. phosphorus Cycle, Sulphur Cycle Iron Cycle, Calcium Cycle

Sedimentary Cycle:-

Sedimentary cycles include the leaching of minerals and salts from the earth's crust which the settle as sediments or rocks before the cycle repeats.

1. Sedimentary cycle includes Phosphorus Cycle
2. Sulphur cycle
3. Iron Cycle
4. Calcium Cycle

Sedimentary cycles vary from one element to another, but each cycle consists fundamentals of a solution phase and a sediment phase.

Water Cycle also known as Hydrological Cycle or the Hydrogeological Cycle describes the continuous flow of water between hydrosphere, atmosphere and lithosphere.

Hydrosphere, atmosphere and lithosphere of water are regularly included in the water cycle or hydrological cycle. Water reaches in the atmosphere through evaporation from seas, lakes, rivers, soil moisture and transpiration from plants etc. and according to changing climatic conditions condenses in the form of clouds and again reaches the hydrosphere and lithosphere.This cyclical movement of water in different forms is called hydrological cycle.

The mass of mass of water on Earth remains fairly constant over time but the partitioning of the water into the major reservoirs of ice, fresh water, saline water and atmospheric water is variable depending on a wide range of climatic variables.

Water cycle is essential for the maintenance of most life and ecosystems on the planet.

Water is a cyclic resource as it is used and re-used.

About 71% of the planetary water is found in the oceans. the remaining is held as fresh water in glaciers and ice-caps, groundwater sources, lakes ,soil moisture, atmosphere, streams and within life.

About 59% of the water on the land surface evaporates and return back to the atmosphere.

The hydrological cycle begins with the evaporation of water from the surface of the ocean.

Steps of Water Cycle

The sun heat causes evaporation of water vapour. When the water vapour cools down, it condenses and forms clouds, from there it may fall on the land or sea in the form of rain, snow.

The process by which water continuously changes its form and circulates between ocean, atmosphere and land is known as the water cycle (Hydrological cycle).

Water Storage in ocean	➢ Evaporation ➢ Transpiration ➢ sublimation
Water in the atmosphere	➢ Condensation ➢ precipitation
Water storage in ice and snow	Snow melt runoff to streams
Surface water runoff	Stream flow freshwater Storage infiltration
Ground water storage	Groundwater discharge springs

Evaporation

The process of conversion of water from liquid to gas stage as it moves from the ground/bodies of water into the atmosphere.

The source of energy for evaporation is mainly solar radiation

Liquid → Gas/Vapour

Transpiration: Water vapour is also discharged from plant leaves by a process called transpiration

Sublimation: The process in which solid water such as snow/ice directly changes into water vapour.

Ice/solid→ water vapour

Condensation: The transformation of water vapour to liquid water droplets in the air, forming fog and clouds

Water vapour → Fog/Cloud

Precipitation: The condensed water vapour falling to the surface of the earth is known as precipitation. It occurs in the form of rain, snow and hail.

Runoff: Runoff is a visible flow of water in rivers, creeks and lakes as the water stored in the basis drain out.

Snowmelt: The runoff created by melting snow.

Percolation: Water flows vertically through the soil and rocks under the effect of gravity.

Infiltration: During infiltration water fills the process spaces on the lithosphere.

Left over water goes as surface runoff

It is pulled downhill because of gravity

Water flows over land and forms rivers. Rivers flow into the ocean and the water cycle continues.

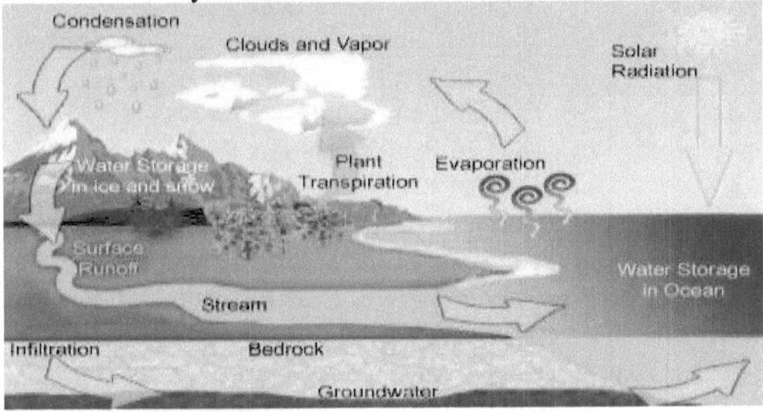

Fig.1.8. Water Cycle

1.7 Biogeographical classification of India

Biogeography deals with the geographical distribution of plants and animals.

Biogeographic zones were used as a basis for planning wildlife protected areas in India.

There are 10 biogeographic zones which are distinguished clearly in India. They are as follows:

1. Trans-Himalayas 2. Himalayas 3. Desert 4.Semi-arid 5.Western Ghats 6. Deccan Peninsula 7. Gangetic plain 8. North-east India 9. Islands 10. Coasts

Bio-geographic Province

Bio-geographic Province is an ecosystematic or biotic sub-division of realms. India is divided into 25 bio geographic zones.

Bio-geographic Zones of India	Bio-Geographic Provinces of India
Trans Himalaya	1A: Himalaya- Ladakh Mountains 1B: Himalaya-Tibetan Plateau 1C: Trans-Himalaya Sikkim
The Himalaya	2A: Himalaya- North West Himalaya 2B: Himalaya- West Himalaya 2C: Himalaya- Central Himalaya 2D: Himalaya- East Himalaya
The Indian Desert	3A: Desert-Thar 3B: Desert-Katchchh
The Western Ghats	4A: Western Ghats-Malabar Plains 5B: Western Ghats- Western Ghats Mountains
The Deccan Peninsula	6A: Deccan Peninsular-Central Highlands 6B: Deccan Peninsular- Chotta Nagpur 6C: Deccan Peninsular- Eastern Highland 6D: Deccan Peninsular- Central Plateau 6E: Deccan Peninsular- Deccan South
The Gangetic Plains	7A: Gangetic Plain- Upper Gangetic Plains 7B: Gangetic Plain- Lower Gangetic Plains
The Coasts	A: Coasts-West Coast 8B: Coasts- East Coast 8C: Coasts-Lakshadweep

North-East India	9A: North-East- East- Brahmaputra Valley 9B: North-East-North East Hills
Islands	10A: Islands-Andaman 10B: Islands-Nicobar

1.Trans-Himalayan Region

The Himalayan ranges immediately north of the Great Himalayan range are called the Trans-Himalayas.

The Trans Himalayan regions of the states of Jammu and Kashmir and Himachal Pradesh are a moonscape land – an arid high altitude desert unlike any other part of the Indian subcontinent.

The stark landscape is a panorama of high snow capped peaks and bare multi hued hills sculpted by the forces of nature.

The high dusty valleys strewn with rock have altitudes ranging from 2,500m to 4,500m.

The Trans-Himalayan region with its sparse vegetation has the richest wild sheep and goat community in the world.

The snow leopard is found here, as is the migratory black-necked cranes.

Trans-Himalayan are divided into four ranges namely,

i. Ladakh range

ii. Zaskar range

iii. Karakoram range

iv. Kailash range.

Trans Himalaya was named by Swedish explorer Sven Hedin.

2.Himlalayas

The Himalayas consist of the youngest and loftiest mountain chains in the world.

The forests are very dense with extensive growth of grass and evergreen tall trees,oak, chestnut, conifer, ash, pine, deodar are abundant in Himalayas.

There is no vegetation above the snowline. Several interesting animals live in the Himalayan ranges.

Chief species include wild sheep, mountain goats,shrew, and tapir. Panda and snow leopard are also found here.(Himalayas are divided into three ranges namely,

 i) Greater Himalaya/Inner Himalaya/Himadri

ii) Lesser Himalaya/Middle Himalaya/Himachal
iii) Outer Himalaya(Shiwaliks)
The Himalayas form a mountain range in Asia. It separates the plains of the Indian subcontinent from the Tibetan Plateau.)

3. Desert: North-West Desert Regions

The Extremely arid area west of the Aravalli hill range, comprising both the salty desert Gujarat and the sand desert of Rajasthan.

This region consists of parts of Rajasthan, Kutch, Delhi and parts of Gujarat.

The climate is characterised by very hot and dry summer and cold winter. Rainfall is less than 70 cm.

The plants are mostly xerophytic. Babul, Kikar, wild palm grows in areas of moderate rainfall.

Indian Bustard, a highly endangered bird is found here. Camels, wild asses, foxes, and snakes are found in hot and arid desert.

4. Semi-Arid Areas

Adjoining the desert are the semi-arid areas, a transitional zone between the desert and the denser forests of the Western Ghats.

The natural vegetation is thorn forest. This region is characterized by discontinuous vegetation cover with open areas of bare soil and soil-water deficit throughout the year.

A few species of xerophytic herbs and some ephemeral herbs are found in this semi-arid tract. Birds, jackals, leopards, eagles, snakes, fox, buffaloes are found in this region.

5. Western Ghats

The mountains along the west coast of peninsular India are the Western Ghats, which constitute one of the unique biological regions of the world.

The Western Ghats extend from the southern tip of the peninsula (8°N) northwards about 1600 km to the mouth of the river Tapti (21°N).

The mountains rise to average altitudes between 900 and 1500 m above sea level,

Apart from biological diversity, the region boasts of high levels of cultural diversity, as many indigenous people inhabit its forests.

The Western Ghats are amongst the **36 biodiversity hot-spots recognized globally**. These hills are known for their high levels of endemism expressed at both higher and lower taxonomic levels. Most of the Western Ghat endemic plants are associated with evergreen forests.

Rice cultivation in the fertile valley proceeded gardens of early commercial crops like areca nut and pepper.

The Western Ghats are well known for harboring 14 endemic species of caecilians (i.e., legless amphibians) out of 15 recorded from the region so far.

The western Ghats is formed by the Malabar Plains and the Chain of Mountains running parallel to Indias Western coast,pass through the state of Gujarat,Maharashtra,Goa,Karnataka,Kerela and Tamil Nadu.(lie along Arabian sea)

6. Deccan Plateau

Beyond the Ghats is Deccan Plateau, a semi-arid region lying in the rain shadow of the Western Ghats.

This is the largest unit of the Peninsular Plateau of India.

The highlands of the plateau are covered with different types of forests, which provide a large variety of forest products.

Fauna like tiger, sloth bear, wild boar, gaur, sambar and chital are found throughout the zone along with small relict populations of wild buffaloes, elephants and barasingha.

Anaimudi is the highest peak of this region.

The Deccan plateau is surrounded by the western and the eastern ghats.These ghats meet each other at the Nilgiri Hills.

The Western Ghats includes the Sahyadri, Nilgiris, Anamalai, and cardamom Hills.

Many rivers such as Mahanadi, Godavari, Krishna, and Kaveri originates from the Western Ghats and flow toward the east.

The Eastern Ghats are broken into small hill ranges by rivers coming from the Western Ghats.

Most of these rivers fall into the Bay of Bengal.

The Godavari is the longest river in the Deccan plateau.

The Narmada and the Tapi flow westwards and fall into the Arabian sea.

7. Gangetic Plain

In the North is the Gangetic plain extending up to the Himalayan foothills. This is the largest unit of the Great Plain of India.

Ganga is the main river after whose name this plain is named.

The Great Plains cover about 72.4mha area with the Ganga and the Brahmaputra forming the main drainage axes in the major portion.

The physiogeographic scenery varies greatly from arid and semi-arid landscapes of the Rajasthan Plains to the humid and per-humid landscapes of the Delta and Assam valley in the east.

The plain supports some of the highest population densities depending upon purely agro-based economy in some of these areas.

The trees belonging to these forests are teak, sal, shisham, mahua, khair etc.

8. North-East India

North-east India is one of the richest flora regions in the country.

It has several species of orchids, bamboos, ferns and other plants.

Here the wild relatives of cultivated plants such as banana, mango, citrus and pepper can be grown

9.Islands

Besides mainland, India territory also extends into Arabian sea form Lakshadweep and the Bay of Bengal form Andaman and Nicobar Island.

Lakshadweep Islands and Kerala Coast. All the Islands in the Arabian Sea are coral Islands and are surrounded by Coral reefs.

The Arabian Sea Islands (Laccadive, Minicoy, etc.) are the foundered remnants of the old land mass and subsequent coral formations.

The island forests of Lakshadweep in the Arabian Sea have some of the best-preserved evergreen forests of India.

Some of the islands are fringed with coral reefs. Many of them are covered with thick forests and some are highly dissected.

10. Coasts

India has a coastline extending over **7516.6 km**.

India has 9 coastal state i.e Gujarat, Maharashtra, Goa, Karnataka, Kerela, Tamil Nadu, Andhar Pradesh, Odisha, West Bengal.

Indian has two coastal plain. The coastal Plain stretching along the Bay of Bengal coast is called "Eastern Coastal Plain" while the one stretching along the Arabian Sea coast is called the western coastal plain.

Western Coastal plain are the example of Submerged coastal plain. And Eastern Coastal plain has emerged coastal plain. For agricultural point of view Eastern coastal plain is more important.

Extensive deltas of the Godavari, Krishna and Kaveri are the characteristic features of this coast. Mangrove vegetation is characteristic of estuarine tracts along the coast for instance, at Ratnagiri in Maharashtra. Larger parts of the coastal plains are covered by fertile soils on which different crops are grown. Rice is the main crop of these areas. Coconut trees grow all along the coast.

1.8. Concept of Biodiversity

Walter G.Rosen coined the termed Biodiversity in **1985.**

Biodiversity derived from the Greek words 'Bios' means Life, and Latin words 'Diversities' means Variety/Difference.

Biodiversity refers to the variety and the numbers of living organisms presents in an ecosystem.

It includes all living things like plants, animals, humans and other organisms (microbes, fungi and invertebrates.

According to United Nation Earth Summit 1992, *Biodiversity is defined as "the variability among living organisms from all sources including, terrestrial, marine and other aquatic ecosystems and the ecological complexes of which they are part, this includes diversity within species between species and of ecosystems".*

Levels of Biodiversity:-

Biological diversity is often understood at three levels: genetic, species and ecosystems.

a. **Genetic Diversity:** The variation of genetic material within a species (or) a population.

Genetic diversity allows species to adapt to changing environment.

The survival of individuals ensures the survival of the population.

The genetic diversity gives us beautiful butterflies, roses, corals in a myriad hues, shapes and sizes.

It helps in speciation or evolution of new species.

It occurs within species or between species.

b. Species Diversity

The number and abundance of species present in different communities.

It refers to the variety of different species on earth (plants, animals, fungi and micro-organisms like bacteria, virus etc.

Species differ from one another, markedly in their genetic makeup, do not inter-breed in nature.

Species diversity is the variety in the number and richness of the species of a region.

The number of species per unit area is called **Species Richness**.

Number of individuals of different species represent **species evenness**

Species diversity is the products of both species evenness.

In India Western Ghats have the greater number of amphibian species diversity as compared to Eastern Ghats.

c. Ecosystem Diversity:

The variety of terrestrial and aquatic ecosystem found in an area (or) on the earth.

It refers to the different types of habitats. A habitat is the cumulative factor of the climate, vegetation and geography of a region. There is several kinds of habitats around the world. Corals, grasslands, wetlands, desert, mangrove and tropical rain forests are examples of ecosystems.

Change in climatic conditions is accompanied by a change in vegetation as well. Each species adapts itself to a particular kind of environment.

Ecological Diversity:

It is related to the different types of ecosystem or habitats. Example: terrestrial (forest, grassland, desert etc), and aquatic ecosystem (fresh water and marine ecosystem).

The ecosystem diversity has three types

   i. Alpha Diversity

   ii. Beta-Diversity

   iii. Gamma Diversity

i. Alpha Diversity (α-Diversity): It represents the number of species found in a community

ii. Beta Diversity(β-Diversity): The rate of turnover i.e incoming movement and outgoing movement of the species from one habitat to another within a given(same) geographical area

iii. Gamma-Diversity(γ-Diversity)

This is the rate of turnover or replacement of species between similar habitats in different geographical area.

1.9. Values of Biodiversity

Biodiversity is valuable natural resources for the survival of mankind. Man has domesticated a number of economically important plants and animal's species.

Old traditional varieties and the mid relatives of domesticated plants and animals constitute a vital genetic resources for us. Many plants and animals including wildlife are of very important for human being. They can be used directly or indirectly to have consumptive, productive, social, ethical, aesthetic and optional values i.e in terms of money.

Biodiversity values are divided into:-

A) Direct values and B) Indirect values.

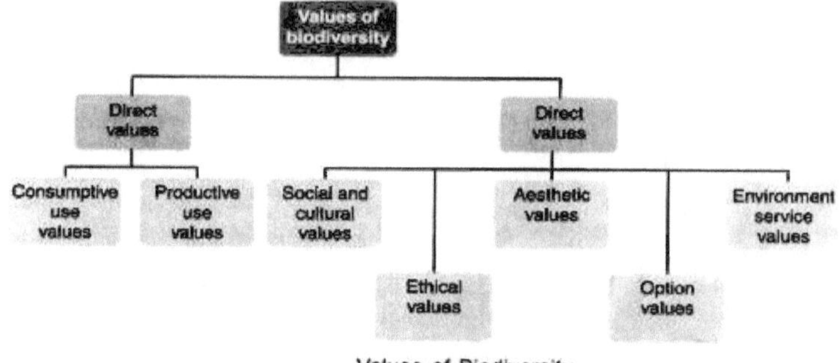

Fig.1.9. Values of Biodiversity

A. Direct Values	B. Indirect Values.
i) Consumptive use values ii) Productive use values	i) Social and cultural values ii)Ethical Values iii)Aesthetic values iv)Option values v)Environmental Service values

A. Direct Values or Ecological and Economic Values

Direct values are also known as ecological or economic values.

Direct value includes food resources like grains, vegetables, fruits which are obtained from plants resources and meat, fish, eggs, milk and milk products from animals resources. These also include other values like medicine, fuel, timber, fibre, wool, wax, resin and rubber, silk etc.

Direct values are two types

i) Consumptive use value

These are the direct use values where the biodiversity products can be harvested and consumed directly such as food, fuel and drugs.

a. Food and Fuel:

The most fundamental value of biological resources particularly plants is providing food. Basically three crops i.e., wheat, maize and rice constitute more than two third of the food requirements all over the world. Most of the developing countries obtain fuel wood from forests. Still more than 1500 million people cook their food by burning wood. Since the forests have provided wood which is used as fuel. Moreover fossil fuels like coal, petroleum, and natural gas are also product of biodiversity which are directly consumed by humans.

b. Drugs and medicines.

Many drugs are derived from plants. Some plants have been found to have immense medicinal properties, few of them with curative properties are given below-

Medicinal Plant	Medicinal part	Curable property
Cinchona Isabgoal	Quinene husk and seed of Isabgoal	Treatment of malaria,Lazative useful in chronic diarrhea,and dysentery.
Opium poppy	Morphine,codeine and narcotine	Mental problems and cough
Brahmi	Juice of leaves and stems	Repairs loss of memory
Ashwagandha(Rau volfia serpentine	Serpentine	Urine problems

ii) Productive Use values.

These are the direct use values where the products is commercially sold in market i.e Productive use value is the value put on the products of nature which are consumed after passing through a market. For example, if we buy fish from the market then it will have productive use value.

B.Indirect Values:

These are those ways by which we don't physically use a plant or animal, but by virtue of its existence it provides services that keep the ecosystem healthy. Indirect values would include social and cultural values, ethical or moral value aesthetic value, option value and scientific or environmental service value.

i) Social and Cultural Value

Many plants and animals are considered holy and sacred in India and are worshipped like Tulsi, cow, snake etc. In Indian society great cultural value is given to forest and as such tiger, peacock and lotus are named as the national animals, birds and flower respectively.

ii) Ethical and moral values:

Every species has its moral right to exist on earth. Every human culture, religion and society has its own ethical values. There are several cultural, moral and ethical values, which are associated with the conservation of biodiversity. We have in our country a large number of sacred grooves or deolis preserved by tribal people in several States. These sacred groves around ancient sacred sites and temples act as gene banks for wild plant

iii)Aesthetic value:

The beauty of our planet is because of biodiversity, which otherwise would have resembled other barren planets dotted around the universe. Biological diversity adds to the quality of life and provides some of the most beautiful aspects of our existence. Biodiversity is responsible for the beauty of a landscape.

People go far off places to enjoy the natural surroundings and wildlife. This type of tourism is referred to as eco-tourism, which has now become a major source of income in many countries. In many societies, the diversity of flora and fauna has become a part of the traditions and culture of the region and has added to the aesthetic values of the place.

iv) Option value:

There are many plants and animals which have not yet been discovered or even if they have been discovered we do not know if they can be of any use to us. This untapped potential is referred to as option value. For example, there might be a plant or animal which we can use in the future to find a cure for corner. If we destroy biodiversity then we lose this chance of finding a cure for cancer. Thus, biodiversity has great potential of being useful to us in the future.

v) Environmental Service values.

a) Protection of water resources
b) Soils formation and protection
c) Nutrients storage and recycling
d) Pollution breakdown and absorption
e) Contribution of climate stability
f) Recovery from unpredictable

1.10. Need for public awareness towards conservation

Planning of a suitable strategy for the conservation of our natural resources and most judicious execution pf planned strategies is called as conservation Management. Environmental planning, evaluation, monitoring and impact assessment are methods of conservation management. The Indian philosophy of conservations is to keep "Harmony with Nature".

Therefore, we have to learn to live with nature. For this every Individual has to play his role to conserve the nature & Nature resources.

It should not be optional but for all i.e old, young, rich, poor, industrialist, common man, consumer, businessman, resident of a colony, wards, slum dweller. Everyone should take part in this work. voluntary organisations are doing some work in this regards but it is not sufficient. Some important roles of individuals in maintaining peace, harmony and equity in nature are as:

i. People should at once stop the over utilization of natural resources instead they must be properly used.

2. Instead of deforestation, representation should keep in mind. We should take help from the Govt. for plantation programmes. Everybody should take part in plantation and care the plants.

3.We should protect wildlife. Though hunting is not allowed even then the persons are doing so. For this educated youth should teach the lessons of wild life act.

4.Mixed cropping, crop rotation, and proper use of fertilizers insecticides, pesticides should be taught to farmers. Encourage the use of manure, biofertilizers and organic fertilizers.

5.We should make habit for waste disposal compose and to restore biodiversity.

6.Try to educate local people for the protection and judicious use of natural resources.

7.Install rain water harvesting system in houses, colonies.

8.We should recycle the waste and waste water for agriculture purposes.

9.We must develop energy saving methods to avoid wastage of energy. We should remember energy saved is energy produced.

10.Utilize renewable energy sources as much as possible. Encourage use of solar cookers, pumps etc.

UNIT TWO
NATURAL RESOURCES

2.1. Natural resources

Resources that are derived directly from nature are **called natural resources.**

Natural resources can be defined as –things/material of nature, that can be put to some use by human beings for their growth, development, and other necessaries are **called as Natural Resources".**

For example, air, water, soil, forests, animals, minerals, metals, energy and other substances are some examples of natural resources that are utilized by human beings.

The resources are not equally distributed throughout the world. We can realize the value of resources only when it is rather scarce. Over exploitation threatens most of our natural resources now.

2.2.Types of Natural resources

There are many ways to classifying these natural resources.

They can be

1. Biotic (that is derived from organic materials, living things, example, plants animals) and

2. Abiotic (that is derived from inorganic materials, example, sunlight, soil water).

Another ways is resources can be classified into exhaustible and in exhausted natural resources on the bases of replenishment

1.Inexhaustible natural resources:

2.Exhaustible natural resources-

1. Inexhaustible natural resources are those which can not be exhausted through continuous use or misuse e.g., **air, and sunlight,** etc.

2. **Exhaustible natural resources** are those which are present in a limited quantity in nature and get exhausted or depleted by human activities

They are further classified into two- Renewable and non-renewable resources.

a) Renewable Natural Resources

Renewable resources are the resources which are available in unlimited quantity and can be used repeatedly. The rate of renewable of these resources is usually faster than the rate of consumption of these resources. Some of the resources, **like sunlight, air, wind, water, land, forest, hydropower etc, are continuously available.**

The natural resources like water, land and forest though are considered as renewable resources but now their quantity is getting noticeably depleted by human consumption. These resources are either getting depleted at an alarming high rate or are being deteriorated by various human activities.

b. Non-renewable resources:

Resources which once used/consumed will never return back **example like coal, petroleum, natural gas etc**. It is important to conserve non-renewable resources, because if we use them too quickly there will not be enough of them left for us for future use. The non-renewable resources cannot be recycled. For example minerals oil, coal and other non-renewable resources cannot be recycled.

2.3. Use and overexploitation of natural resources

i) The main problem associated with natural resources is unequal consumption.

ii) A major part of natural resources are consumed in the 'developed' world. The 'developing nations' also over use many resources because of their greater human population. However, the consumption of resources per capita (per individual) of the developed countries is up to 50 times greater than in most developing countries.

iii) Advanced countries produce over 75% of global industrial waste and greenhouse gases.

iv) Energy from fossil fuels consumed in relatively much greater quantities in developed countries. Their per capita consumption of food too is much greater as well as their waste

Forest Resources: A forest can be defined as a biotic community predominant of trees, shrubs or any other woody vegetation usually in a closed canopy.

Functions of Forest

1. It performs very important function both to human and to nature.
2. They are habitats to millions of plants, animals and wild life.
3. They recycle rain water.
4. They remove pollutant from air.
5. They control water quality.
6. They moderate temperature and weather.
7. They influence soil condition and prevent soil erosion.

Uses of forest

1. Commercial uses 2. Ecological uses

1. **Commercial uses:**

i. Wood – used as a fuel

ii. Supply wood for various industries – Raw materials as pulp, paper, furniture timber etc.

iii. Minor forest products – gum, dyes, resins

iv. Many plants – Medicines

v. Supply variety of animal products – honey. Ivory, horns etc.

vi. Many forest lands are used for - Mining, grazing, for dams and recreation.

2. Ecological uses: Forest provides number of environmental services.

i. **Production of oxygen:** Photosynthesis produces large amount of oxygen which is essential for life.

ii. **Reducing global warming:** Carbon dioxide is one of the main green house gas. It is absorbed by plants for photosynthesis. Therefore the problem of global warming caused by CO2 is reduced.
iii. **Soil conservation:** Roots of trees bind the soil tightly and prevent soil erosion. They also act as wind breaks.
iv. **Regulation of hydrological cycle:** Watershed in forest act like giant sponges and slowly release the water for recharge of spring

2.4.   Over exploitation of forest

Due to over population, there is an increased demand for medicine, shelter, wood and fuel. Hence exploitation of forest materials is going on increasing.

Cause of over exploitation:
1. Increasing agricultural production.
2. Increasing agricultural activities.
3. Increase in demand of wood resources

Deforestation: It is process of removal of forest resources due to natural or manmade activities (i.e.) destruction of forests.

Causes of deforestation:
1. **Developmental projects:** Developmental projects causes deforestation through two ways.
  Through submergence of forest area.
  Destruction of forest area.
  Ex: big dams, hydro electric projects, road construction etc.
2. **Mining operations:** It reduces forest areas. Ex: Mica, coal, Manganese and lime stone.
3. **Raw materials for industries:** Wood is an important raw material for various purposes.
   Ex: Making boxes, furniture and paper etc.
4. **Fuel requirement:** Wood is the important fuel for rural and tribal population
5. **Shifting cultivation:** Replacement of natural forest ecosystem for mono specific tree plantation. Ex: Teak
6. **Forest fires:** Forest fire destructs thousands of acres of forest.
7. **Over grazing:** Over grazing by cattle reduces the cultivation land

Consequences of deforestation:
1. Economic loss
2. Loss of biodiversity
3. Destructs the habitats of various species
4. Reduction in stream flow
5. Increases the rate of global warming
6. Disruption of weather patterns and global climate
7. Degradation of soil and acceleration of the rate of soil erosion.
8. Induces and accelerates mass movement / land slides.
9. Increases flood frequency, magnitude / severity.
10. Breaks the water cycle
11. Breaks the nutrient cycle

Preventive measures
1. New plants of more or less of the same variety should be planted to replace the trees cut down for timber
2. Use of wood for fuel should be discouraged.
3. Forest pests can be controlled by spraying pesticides by using aero planes
4. Forest fire must be controlled by modern techniques.

2.5. Water resources

Water resources are sources of water that are useful or potentially useful. Uses of water include agricultural, industrial, household, recreational and environmental activities. Virtually all of these human uses require fresh water.

Distribution of water on earth:
97% of the water on the Earth is salt water. Only three percent is fresh water; slightly over two thirds of this is frozen in glaciers and polar ice. The remaining unfrozen freshwater is found mainly as groundwater, with only a small fraction present above ground or in the air.

Fresh water occurs mainly in two forms
1. Ground water and 2. Surface water
1. Groundwater: About 9.86% of the total fresh water resources is in the form of ground water and it is about 35-50 times that of surface water supplied.

Use of water
1. Domestic use: Water used in the houses for the purposes of drinking, bathing,
washing Clothes, cooking, sanitary & other needs. The recommended value according to
Indian standard specification for domestic use is 135 liters/day
2. Industrial use: Water is required for various industries such as cement, mining, textile, leather industries.
3. Public use: This includes water used for public utility purpose such as watering parks, Flushing streets, jails etc.
4. Fire use : Water is used in case of accidents and to prevent the fire issues.
5. Irrigation: To grow crops which is the main sources for food?
6. other uses Hydro electric power generation requires water.

Over utilization of ground water and surface water
Over use of groundwater has following effects.
1. **Lowering of water table:** Excessive use of ground water for drinking, irrigation and Domestic purposes has resulted in rapid depletion of ground water in various regions leading to lowering of water table & drying of wells.
The reasons for shortage of water are:
a. Increase in population,
b. Increasing demand of water for various purposes.
c. Unequal distribution of fresh water.
d. Increasing pollution of water sources cause over exploitation.
2. **Ground subsidence:** When ground water withdrawal is greater than its recharge rate, the sediments in the aquifer become compacted. This is called ground subsidence which may cause damage of buildings, destroy water supply systems etc.
3. **Drought. A drought** is an extended period of months or years when a region notes a deficiency in its water supply whether surface or underground water. Generally, this occurs when a region receives consistently below average precipitation.

We can define drought in four main ways:
a) Meteorological drought: related to rainfall amounts
b) Hydrological drought: determined by water levels in reservoirs

c) Agricultural drought: related to the availability of water for crops

d) Socioeconomic Drought: related to demand and supply of economic goods

a) Meteorological Drought: Meteorological drought is generally defined by comparing the rainfall in a particular place and at a particular time with the average rainfall for that Place. The definition is, therefore, specific to a particular location. Meteorological drought leads to a depletion of soil moisture and this almost always has an impact on crop production.

b) Hydrological Drought: Hydrological drought is associated with the effect of low rainfall on water levels in rivers, reservoirs, lakes and aquifers. Hydrological droughts usually are noticed some time after meteorological droughts. First precipitation decreases and, Sometime after that, water levels in rivers and lakes drop.

C) Agricultural Drought: Agricultural drought mainly effects food production and farming.

Agricultural drought and precipitation shortages bring soil water deficits, reduced ground water or reservoir levels, and so on. Deficient topsoil moisture at planting may stop germination, leading to low plant populations.

d) Socioeconomic Drought: Socioeconomic drought occurs when the demand for an economic good exceeds supply as a result of a weather-related shortfall in water supply. The supply of many economic goods, such as water, forage, food grains, fish, and hydroelectric power, depends on weather. Due to variability of climate, water supply is sufficient in some years but not satisfactory to meet human and environmental needs in other year.

2.6 Mineral resources

Naturally occurring inorganic crystalline solids with uniform chemical composition are called as minerals.

Uses and exploitation of minerals

1. Development of industrial plants and machinery. - Fe, Al & Cu
2. Construction work – Fe, Al &Ni
3. Generation of energy - coal, lignite, uranium
4. Designing defense equipments like weapons and ornaments

5. Agricultural purposes – fertilizers and fungicides – Zn & Mn
6. Jewelry –Au, Ag & Pt
7. Making alloys for various purposes
8. Communication purposes – telephone, wires, cables and electronic devices
9. Medicinal purposes, particularly in ayurvedic system

Environmental Damages caused by Mining activities
1. Devegetation:
i)Topsoil and vegetation get removed
ii) Deforestation leads to several ecological losses
iii) Land scape gets badly affected
2. Ground water contamination: Mining pollutes ground water; sulphur is converted into sulphuric acid which enters into the soil.
3. Surface water pollution: Radioactive wastes and other acidic impurities affect the surface water, which kills many aquatic animals.
4. Air pollution: Smelting and roasting are done to purify the metal which emits air pollutants and damage the nearby vegetation. It causes many health problems.
5. Subsidence of land: Mainly underground mining results in cracks in houses, tilting of buildings and bending of rail tracks.

Effects of Over exploitation of Mineral
1. Rapid depletion of mineral deposits
2. Wastage
3. Environmental pollution
4. Needs heavy energy requirements

Management of Mineral resources:
1. The efficient use and protection of mineral resources.
2. Modernization of mining industries
3. Search for new deposit
4. Reuse and recycling of the metals.
5. Environmental impacts can be minimized by adopting eco-friendly mining technology.

2.7.Role of an Individual in conservation of natural resources

Different natural resources like forests, water, soil, food, mineral and energy resources play a vital role in the development of a nation. With our small individual efforts, we can together help in conserving our natural resources to a large extent.

Following are the ways:
a) Conserve Water:
1. Don't keep water taps running while brushing, shaving, washing or bathing.
2. In washing machines fill the machine only to the level required for your clothes.
3. Install water saving toilets that use not more than 6 liters per flush.
4. Check for water leaks in pipes and toilets and repair them promptly.
5. Reuse the soapy water of washing from clothes for gardening, driveways etc.
6. Water the plants and the lawns in the evening when evaporation losses are minimum. Never water the plants in mid-day.
7. Install a system to capture rain water.

b) Conserve energy:
1. Turn off lights fans and other appliances when not in use.
2. Obtain as much heat as possible from natural sources. Dry the clothes in sun instead of direr if possible.
3. Use solar cooker for cooking which will be more nutritious and will save your LPG Expenses.
4. Build your house with provision for sunspace which will keep your house warmer and will provide more light.
5. Drive less, make fewer trips and use public transportations whenever possible. Share a car-pool if possible.
6. Control the use of A.C.
7. Recycle and reuse glass, metals and papers.
8. Use bicycle or just walk down small distances instead of using vehicle.

Protect the Soil:
1. Grow different types of ornamental plants, herbs and trees in your garden. Grow grass in the open areas which will bind the soil and prevent its erosion.
2. Make compost from your kitchen waste and use it for your kitchen-garden.
3. Do not irrigate the plants using a strong flow of water as it would wash off the soil.
4. Better use sprinkling irrigation.

Promote Sustainable Agriculture:
1. Do not waste food; Take as much as you can eat.
2. Reduce the use of pesticides.
3. Fertilize your crop with organic fertilizers.
4. Use drip irrigation.
5. Eat local and seasonal vegetables.
6. Control pest.

2.8.Population growth

The population size is the number of individuals in a population at a given time. Even when the population size appears to be stable over time, changes can occur from year to year or from place to place. Population size varies from one habitat to another. It also varies within a single habitat.

Population growth:

Population growth refers to the change in the population over time.

Population growth is determined by the number of individuals added to the population of birth(Natality) and immigration and the number of individual lost from the population due to death (Mortality) and emigration.

Rapid growth of population if called population explosion.

> Population Growth = (Birth+Immigration) – Death- Emigration
>
> $$N_t = N_0 + B + I - D - E$$
>
> N_t = Final population size
> N_0 = Initial population size
> B = Natality
> I = Immigration
> D = Mortality
> E = Emigration
> Natality   : Number of Birth
> Mortality   : Number of Death
> Immigration   : Coming of population into the habitat
> Emmigration : Lost of population who left the habitat.

Demography is the study of human populations, which has various connected issues like, fertility, mortality, migration, public health, work, family and family planning.

According to the 2012 Revision of the United Nations Population estimates and projections, the world population of 7.2 billions in 2013 is projected to increase by almost one billion people within the next twelve years, reaching 8.1 billion in 2025, and to further increase to 9.6 billion in 2050.The rapid growth in population has been called a population explosion.

The main reason of world's population changes is the transformation in birth and death rates. When the birth rate is higher than the death rates, the population grows.

China and India had 37 percent of the world population in 2013 and by 2028, the two countries will account then for about 35 percent of the world population.

Causes of population growth

    a. The rapid population growth is due to decrease in death rate and increase in birth rate(natality)

    b. Availability of antibiotics, immunization, Increased food production, clean water and air decreases the famine-related deaths.

c. In agricultural based countries, children are required to help parents in the field that is why population increases in the developing countries.

d. Causes of population explosion: Modern medical facilities reduces death rate & increases birth rate, Increase of life expectancy,

e. Poverty, Illiteracy leads controlled growth of population

f. Child marriage

g. People's superstitions, People believe that child is the gift from God.

Control the population growth

A very high level of population growth can create imbalances, which make the job of the state more difficult, but the way the issue is being approached is problematic and will have unintended consequences

i. Stop child marriage.

ii. Increase status of women

iii. Spread education to the community for prefer delay marriage and planning small family custom.

iv. Late marriage will reduce the period of reproduction among females and bring down the birth rate.

v. Minimum age of marriage should be implement strongly.

vi. Government should devise more employment apport unity

vii. Employment to women is effective methods to control population.

viii. Urbanization should be encouraged. It is reported in the research that urban areas has low birth rates as compare to rural areas.

2.9. Impact of human population growth on Natural and environment

Population has a deep impact on environment and issues like population explosion has put an increasing on earth and its resources.

The impact of human population growth on nature and the environment is profound and wide-ranging. Some are discussed below:

1.Habitat Loss and fragmentation:

With the increase of human populations, natural habitats are converted for agricultural, industrial, and urban purposes. This leads to habitat loss, fragmentation and degradation, disrupting ecosystems and threatening biodiversity. Species depending on specific habitats may face extension or population declines due to loss of suitable living spaces.

2.Resources Depletion

Increasing human populations require more resources to support food production, energy consumption and infrastructure development. This results in over-exploitation and depletion of natural resources such as freshwater, forests, fisheries, and minerals. Unsustainable resources extraction practices can lead to ecosystem collapse and long-term environmental degradation.

3.Pollution

Human activities associated with population growth including industrialization, transportation, and waste disposal, generate various forms of pollution. Air pollution from vehicle emissions and industrial processes contributes to respiratory diseases and climate change. Water pollution from agricultural runoff, industrial discharge and sewage contamination affects aquatic ecosystems and human health. Soil pollution from pesticides, fertilizers and hazardous wate disposal can degrade land productivity and contaminate food supplies.

4.Climate Change

Human-induced climate change is a significant consequences of population growth and associated greenhouse gas emissions. Burning fossils fuels gas for energy, deforestation, and industrial processes release carbon dioxide and other greenhouse gases into the atmosphere, trapping heat and altering the Earth's climate system. Climate change leads to more frequent and severe weather events rising sea levels, shifts in precipitation patterns and agricultural productivity, posing risks to human societies and natural environments worldwide.

5.Loss of Biodiversity

The expansion of human populations and activities accelerates the loss of biodiversity through habitat destruction pollution, over-exploitation, and the introduction of invasion species. Species extinction rates are increasing due to human-induced pressure, threatening the stability and resilience of ecosystems. Biodiversity loss reduces ecosystem services such as pollination, nutrients cycling and disease regulation, compromising the ability of ecosystems to support human well-being and sustainable development.

6.Social and Economic Impacts:

Population growth can exchange exacerbate social and economic inequalities, as limited resources and environmental degradation disproportionately affects marginalized communities and vulnerable population. Competition for land, water and natural resources can leads to conflicts, displacement and migration with implications for human rights, security and global stability.

Addressing the impacts of human population growth on nature and the environment requires integrated approaches that promote sustainable development, conservation and resilience-building efforts. Strategies may include reducing consumption and waste generation, transitioning to renewable energy resources, implementing ecosystem-based management practices, conserving biodiversity and protected areas, promoting sustainable land use and urban planning and fostering international cooperation and partnerships for environmental stewardship.

2.10. Sustainable Development

Sustainability is derived from the Latin word sustainer i.e., to hold and sustain. Sustain is to maintain. It is related to the quality of life in a community-whether the economic, social and environment systems that make up the community are providing a healthy productive, meaningful life for all community residents, present and future.

Sustainability can be defined as the practice of maintaining processes of productivity (natural or human made) indefinitely by replacing resources used with resources of equal or greater value without degrading or endangered natural biotic systems.

Sustainable development

The concept of sustainable development had two related concepts, i.e., the right to develop and the need to sustain the environment, which need to be balanced for achieving future development in a sustainable manner.

According to Brundtland Commission in its (1987) report "Our Common Future".

"Sustainable development is development that meets the needs of the present, without compromising the ability of future generations to meet their own needs."

Sustainable development has three goals:

i. To minimize the depletion of natural resources,

ii. To promote development without causing harm to the environment and

iii. To make use of environmentally friendly practices.

A few years later,in 1992,representatives from most of the world's countries met in Rio De Janerio,from Brazil,for the U.N conference on   Environment and Development.

The four important dimensions of the sustainability are economic, ecological, political, and cultural sustainability.

The first three domains were endorsed by the United Nations Millennium Declaration i.e., economic, environment and social sustainability. So to achieve true sustainability we need to balance economic, social and environmental sustainability factors in equal harmony.

Rio + 20

In 2012, at the UNCSD United Nations Conference on Sustainable Development taken place in Brazil on 20-22 June, 2012.Here world leaders along with thousands of participants from government, the private sector, NGOs and other groups came together to share how to reduce poverty, advance social equity and ensure environmental protection on an ever more crowded planet to get to 'the future we want'.

Theme of this conference

A green economy in the context of sustainable development and poverty eradication.

The institutional framework for sustainable development.

7 Priority Areas of Rio+20 Conference

Decent Jobs, energy, sustainable cities, food security and sustainable agriculture, water, oceans and disaster readiness.

RIO+5

In 1997,the UN, General Assembly held a special session to appraise the status of Agenda 21.The widening inequalities in income and continued deterioration of the global environment.

RIO+10

The Johannesburg Plan to implementation, agreed at the (WSSD) world summit on sustainable Development(Earth Summit 2002)affirmed UN Commitment to 'full implementation' of Agenda

21,alongside achievement of the Millennium Development Goals and other international agreements.

Agenda 21

It is a non-binding action plan of the United Nations with regards to sustainable development. It is the product of the Earth Summit held in Rio de Janeiro, Brazil, in 1992.

It is a 300 page document divided into 40 chapters that have been grouped into 4 sections:-

Section 1: Social and economic Dimensions is directed toward combating poverty:

Section 2: Conservation and Management of Resources for Development

Section 3:Strengthening the Role of major includes the roles of children and youth, women. NGOs, local authorities, business, and workers and strengthening the role of indigenous people their communities and farmers.

Section 4:Means of implementation.

Implementation include, science ,technology, transfer and education, international institutional and financial mechanism.

Sustainable Development Goals:

on September 25ᵗʰ2015,countries adopted a set of common goal to end proverty,protect the planet and ensure prosperity for all as part of a new sustainable development agenda.Each goal has specific targets to be achieved over the next 15 years.There are a set of 17 'Global Goals' with 169 targets between them

These goals are

1. End poverty in all its forms everywhere
2. End hunger, achieve food security and improved nutrition and promote sustainable agriculture
3. Ensure healthy lives and promote well being for all at all stages

4. Ensure inclusive and equitable quality education and promote lifelong learning opportunities for all
5. Achieve gender equality and empower all women and girls
6. Ensure availability and sustainable management of water and sanitation for all
7. Ensure access to affordable, reliable, sustainable and modern energy for all
8. Promote sustained, inclusive and sustainable economic growth, full and productive employment and decent work for all
9. Built resilient infrastructure, promote inclusive and sustainable industrialization and foster innovation
10. Reduce inequalities within and among countries
11. Make cities and human settlements inclusive, safe, resilient and sustainable
12. Ensure sustainable consumption and production pattern
13. Take urgent actions to combat climate change and its impact
14. Conserve and sustainably use the oceans, seas and marine resources
15. Protect, restore and promote sustainable use of terrestrial ecosystems, sustainably managed forests, combat desertification and halt and reverse land degradation and halt biodiversity loss
16. Promote peaceful and inclusive societies for sustainable development, provide access to justice for all and build effective, accountable and inclusive institutions at all levels
17. Strengthen the means of implementation and revitalise the global partnership for sustainable development

UNIT THREE

ENVIRONMENTAL POLLUTION, LAWS, AND MANAGEMENT

3.1. Environmental Pollution

Any undesirable change in the physical, chemical and biological properties of air, water and land that adversely effect on human and other living organisms in the environment are called **environmental pollution.**

Any substances/agents that cause environmental pollution are called **Pollutant.** Pollutants are the chemicals or substance that causes adversely effect on the natural quality of any component of the environment.

Example: Smokes from industries and Automobile, Chemicals from factories, radioactive substance from nuclear plant, sewage of houses and discharged household articles are the common pollutants.

Classification of Pollutants from an ecological perspective

The pollutants from an ecological points of view can be classified as follows:

i. Degradable/Non-persistent pollutants

These pollutants can be rapidly broken down by natural processes. For example: Discarded vegetables, domestic sewage, etc.

ii) Slowly degradable/Persistent pollutants:

These pollutants remain in the environment for many years in an unaffected condition and take decades or very long time to degrade. For example, DDT and Plastic waste.

iii) Non-Degradable pollutants/Non-Biodegradable Pollutants: pollutants, which are not decomposed or breaking down by the natural process. Example, toxic, heavy metals(lead, mercury) radioactive substance etc

Environmental Pollution is classified into various types as follows:-

1. Air Pollution'	Pollutants of air is termed as air/atmospheric pollutants
2.Noise Pollution	Urban areas are affected with the menace of noise, which at times becomes intolerable. It is called noise pollution
3.Water Pollution	The pollution of hydrosphere/water is called Water Pollution
4.Soil Pollution	Pollution of lithosphere/land, called soil pollution
5.Thermal Pollution	Pollution due to increase in ambient temperature of water
6.Radiation Pollution	Pollution due to harmful radioactive rays/chemical

3.2.Air Pollution

Any undesirable changes in the physical, chemical and biological properties of air, that are adversely, effect on human beings and their natural environment the ultimate result is a change in the natural environment and ecosystem is referred to as air pollution".

According to Air Act 1981 Air Pollution means *"Any solid, Liquid or gaseous substance(including noise) present in the atmosphere in such concentration as may be or tend to be injuries to human beings or other being creatures or plants or property or environment*

Causes of Air Pollution

There are several causes of air pollution and these are discussed here in brief as:

1.Burning of Fossil Fuels:

Sulfur dioxide gas released from the combustion of fossil fuels(coal, petroleum, etc) and other combustibles from factory is one the major cause of air pollution. Emissions from vehicles (trucks, jeeps, cars, trains, airplanes etc) cause massive amount of pollution. Corbon monoxide gas released from vehicles due to improper or incomplete combustion is   another major pollutant along with oxides of nitrogen, which is produced from both natural and man-made processes.

2.Exhaust from factories and industries:

Generally, manufacturing industries release huge amount of carbon monoxide, hydrocarbons, organic compounds and chemicals into the air which deplete the quality of air. Petroleum refineries also discharge hydrocarbons and various other chemical pollutants in the air which cause immense amount of pollution.

3.Agricultural activities:

Agricultural related activities released ammonia as its by product which is one of the most hazardous gases in the atmosphere. Use of insecticides, pesticide and fertilizers in agricultural activities also emit harmful chemicals into the air.

4.Indoor air pollution:

Household cleaning products and painting materials produce toxic chemicals in the air which cause air pollution.

5.Mining operations: During the process of mining, dust and chemicals are released in the air causing considerable air pollution.

6.Suspended Particulate matter(SPM) : It is another cause of pollution, which is generally caused by dust, combustion etc. Diesel exhaust matter air pollution. Particulate matter can be natural such as dust, seeds, spores, pollen grains, algae, fungi, bacteria and viruses and anthropogenic such as mineral dust, cement, asbestos dust, fibres metal dust, fly ash, smoke particles forms fires etc.

Effect of Air Pollution

Depending upon the concentration of air pollutants, several effects can be noticed and are discussed briefly.

1. Effect on Human Health

The effects of sir pollution are frightening as they are known to create several respiratory infections, heart diseases, stroke and lung cancer and other health threats to the body.

Several people die due to direct and indirect effects of air pollution.

Children in areas exposed to air pollutants are commonly suffered from difficulty in breathing, coughing, wheezing, pneumonia, asthma and cardiac conditions.

Sulphur dioxide (SO₂) produced by the **Volcanoes** and in many industrial processes.

It is also produced by combustion of coal and petroleum.

It is presence of NO_2 and SO_2 form H_2SO_4 which causes **acid rain.**

SO_2 causes respiratory diseases.

Nitrogen Dioxide are a produced naturally by **lightning and** It forms HNO_3 and causes photochemical smog, **acid rain etc.,it can irritate respiratory tissues.**

Carbon monoxide poisoning is the most common type of fatal air poisoning.

It is toxic to haemoglobin animals (including humans) when encountered in concentrations above about 35 ppm.

It combines with haemoglobin to produce carboxy-haemoglobin, which usurps the space in haemoglobin that normally carries oxygen. This leads to impaired perception and thinking, and causes headches, dizziness.

Suspended particulate matter in air make worse bronchitis and asthma. Several Volatile organic compound(VOC) such as benzene and toxic particulates such as lead, cadmium etc can cause mutations, reproductive problems or cancer.

2.Effect on Agriculture:

Due to air pollution, crop yields have decreased drastically in India. In 2014, it was reported that air pollution had cut crop yields in the most affected areas in India by almost half in 2010 when compared to 1980 levels.

3.Effect on Plants

Air pollution damage the levels of crop plants due to the entry of gaseous pollutants in leaf pores. Continual exposure of the leaves to air pollutants also break down the waxy coating which helps in preventing excessive water loss and leads to damage from diseases, pests, drought and frost. In addition, such exposure interferes with photosynthesis process and plant growth, thereby reduces nutrient uptake and causes leaves to turn yellow, brown or drop off altogether.

4.Effect on wildlife

Air pollution not only affects humans but animals also suffer from destructive effects of air pollution. Toxic chemicals present in the air can force wildlife species to move to novel place and vary their habitat. The toxic pollutants deposit over the surface of the water and also effect sea animals.

5.Acid Rain

During the burning of fossil fuels, harmful gases like nitrogen oxides(NO_2) and surfur oxides(SO_2) are released into the atmosphere. When it rains, the water droplets present in air combines with these air pollutants (NO_2 and SO_2) and become acidic. Then these falls on the ground in the form of acid rain which causes great damage to human beings, animals and crops.

6.Eutrophication

Eutrophication is increase in amount of plants nutrients Nitrogen and phosphorus(N,P)in water due to detergents, pesticides etc., and leads to organic leading, depletion of Dissolved Oxygen, algae blooms, and died of aquatic animals in water bodies.

Excessive discharge of Nutrients(N.P.K) into water, resulting in accelerated growth of aquatic plants, weeds, invasions species, etc. It leads to algal bloom.

Leads to reduction in the levels of Dissolve Oxygen.

Leads to dead of the aquatic animals present in the water body

7.Effect on climate change: Global warming and Greenhouse effect: Global warming is another direct effect that the world is witnessing due to air pollution.

Greenhouse Gases/Atmospheric gasses such as CO_2, CH_4, N_2O and CFCs present in the atmosphere, which absorbs heat and do not radiate cause increase in atmospheric and global temperature.

It is similar to the warming effect observed in the green house made of green glass, and the heating effect is called **greenhouse effect.**

Green House effect is the heating effect exerted by the atmosphere on the earth due to the presence of certain gases called Green House Gases., water vapour CO_2, CH_4, N_2O and CFCs.

Global Warming Global warming is an average increase in the temperature of the atmosphere near the Earth Surface and in the troposphere, which can contribute to changes in global climate patterns.

Global warming is a gradual increase in the overall temperature of earth's atmosphere, generally attributed to the green house effect caused by the increased levels of GHGs.

Due to increased temperatures worldwide, there is increase in ice-cap, melting of glaciers, Widespread vanishing of animal's populations due to habitat loss, spread of disease (like malaria), Bleaching of coral reefs, Loss of aquatic species due to warming of the water.

If these GHS are not checked properly, there will be more melting of these polar ice-cap which further increase the sea level leading to coastal flooding, loss of coastal areas and ecosystems like, swamps and marshes.

8.Effect on Stratosphere-depletion of ozone layer.

Ozone is a gas made up of three oxygen atoms (O_3). It occurs naturally in small (trace) amounts in the upper atmosphere (the stratosphere). Ozone protects life on Earth from the Sun's ultraviolet (UV) radiation.

Certain chemicals like Chlorofluorocarbons used for refrigerators, air conditioning, fire extinguishers, cleaning solvents, aerosols (spray cans of perfumes, medicine, insecticides etc.) cause damage to ozone layer. Actually, chlorine contained in the CFCs on reaching ozone(O_3) layer split the ozone molecules to form oxygen(O_2).Amount of ozone, thus gets reduced and cannot prevent the entry of UV radiation. There has been reduction of ozone umbrella or shield over the Artic and Antartica regions. This is known as *Ozone Hole.* This permits passage of UV radiation on earth's atmosphere which causes sunburn, cataract in eyes leading to blindness, skin cancer, reduced productivity of forests, also have the tendency to affect crops, etc. Depletion of ozone effects human health badly, UV Rays destroy skin in human, It also effect the aquatic forms, Increases the average temperature of earth, Ecological imbalance(disturbance). It also effects food production, it also contribute to global warming.

Control and Preventive measures of Air Pollution
Important prevention strategies to control Air pollution are:-
Use Public mode of transportation:
We should encourage people to use more and more public mode of transportation in order to reduce air pollution. Furthermore, endeavour to make use a car pooling. If we and our colleagues come from the same locality and have similar timings then we can look at this alternative to save energy as well as money. Using odd even formula in Delhi has given some relief to air pollution problems as well as traffic congestion in the recent year. All Four wheeled vehicles with registration number ending with even digit will not be allowed on odd dates and vice versa. Many people carpooled, while others travelled in autos, bus, metros cabs and public transport.

Set emission standards for automobiles:
The emission standards for automobiles have been set which if followed will reduce the air pollution. Standards have been set for the durability of catalytic converters which decrease vehicular emission. In cities like Delhi motor vehicles need to obtain Pollution Under Control (PUC)Certificate at regular intervals which

ensures that levels of pollutants emitted from vehicles exhaust are not beyond the prescribed legal limits.

Air Quality monitoring:

Air quality monitoring helps in controlling air pollution. Air quality monitoring began in India in the late 1960s which focused only some pollutants like sulphur dioxide, nitrogen oxides and suspended particulate matter. Other pollutants such as carbon monoxide and lead were monitored only on a limited scale. The threat from other air toxins such as benzene, ozone, and other small particulates is not known as these are not monitored at all. Then, central pollution control Board (CPCB) initiated its own national Ambient Air Quality Monitoring (NAAQM) program in 1985.

Control Indoor Air Pollution: Use of wood and dung cakes should be replaced by cleaner fuels such as biogas, kerosene or electricity. The house design should incorporate a well ventilated kitchen or electricity. The encourage people to use biogas and CNG(Compressed Natural Gas).Indoor pollution due to rot of bare kitchen waste can be reduced by covering the waste properly. Segregation of waste, pretreatment at source, sterilization of rooms, etc. can be employed for controlling indoor air pollution.

Control of Industrial Pollution:

In order to control industrial pollution we should use cleaner flues like Liquified Natural Gas (LNG) in power plants, fertilizers plants etc. which is not only environmentally friendly but cheaper too. Employ environment friendly industrial processes in order to minimize the emission of pollutants and hazardous waste. There are certain devices like filters, inertia collectors, electrostatic precipitators, scrubbers, dry scrubbers or gravel bed filters which reduce release of pollutants. We should install these devices.

Emphasis on clean energy resources: Clean sources of energy like solar, wind and geothermal must be used. Governments should providing grants to consumers who are interested in installing solar panels at their home. In this way, air pollution can be controlled for long term.

Understand the concept of 3R:
Do not throw away items that are of no use. In facts, reuse them for some further purpose.

Use energy efficient devices:
CFL lights consume less electricity compared to their counterparts. These can live longer; consume less electricity so lower electricity bills and also help to reduce pollution by consuming less energy.

3.2. Water Pollution

The presence of any foreign substance (inorganic, organic, biological or radioactive) which alters the physical, chemical and biological properties of water which constitutes a health hazard or decreases the usefulness of water is termed as water pollution.

Water pollution is the contamination of water bodies (e.g. lakes, rivers, oceans, aquifers and groundwater). This form of environmental degradation occurs when pollutants are directly or indirectly discharged into water bodies without adequate treatment to remove harmful compounds.

Point sources and Non-Point sources water pollution

1. Point Sources
When contamination originates from a single sources, its called point sources pollution

Point sources are discharged pollutants at specific locations through pipes, diches or sewers into bodies of water.

- ➢ Effluent(waste water) discharged from sewage treatment
- ➢ Industrial effluents
- ➢ Oil storage facilities
- ➢ Fish farming

2. Non-Point/Diffused Sources:

Pollutants which doesn't release from a single point or whose source is unknown.

They cannot be traced to any single sites of discharge.

They are usually large land areas or air sheds that pollute water by runoff, subsurface flow or deposition from the atmosphere

Pesticides use, organic waste recycling land, agricultural fertilizers, Power generation

Causes of water Pollution

1.Industrial effluents

Most industrial effluents are discharged into rivers. These contain both organic and inorganic hazardous materials and non-biodegradable one too. Industries produce huge amount of waste which contains toxic chemicals and pollutants such as lead, cadmium, mercury, sulphur, nitrate and many other chemicals which drained in the fresh water which goes into rivers.

2.Municipal sewage

Most municipal sewages receive no treatment before discharge. These in combination with industrial wastes pose new public health problem. It is a point to be noted that since population growth is increasing the quantity of waste water is also increasing in addition to the production of large quantities of sewage.

Common organic materials found in sewage are soaps, synthetic detergents, fatty acids, esters, amines, amino acids etc.It also contain numerous micro-organisms, some of which may be pathogenic in character.

3. Agricultural Practices.

Chemical fertilizers and pesticides are used by farmers for protecting crops from insects and pests. But when these chemicals are mixed with water, they are harmful for plants and animals. In addition, when it rains, these chemicals mixes up with rainwater and flow down into rivers and canals and cause serious damage to aquatic animals.

4.Animal waste

The waste generated by animals is washed away into the rivers by rain and gets mixed with other harmful chemicals and cause various water borne diseases such as diarrhoea, cholera, jaundice, typhoid and dysentery.

5.Leakage from the landfills.

Landfills are giant pile of garbage that produces unpleasant smell and can be seen across the city. When it rains, the landfills may leak and the leaking landfills can pollute the underground water with large variety of contaminants.

6. Urban Development

Due to increase in population, the demand for housing, food and clothing has also increased. As more cities and towns are developed, they have resulted in soil erosion due to deforestation, increase use of fertilizers for more food production, increase in construction activities, inadequate sewer treatment, landfills, increase in chemicals from industries to produce more materials and hence more pollution.

7.Global warming

An increase in earth's temperature due to greenhouse effect results in global warming. It increases the water temperature and result in death of aquatic animals and marine species which afterward results in water pollution

8.Radioactive substance

Radioactive substances enters into water bodies through several sources like mining and radioactive plants involving the refining of Uranium and Thorium, disposal of nuclear waste.

Medical and scientific research facilities also use them- eg. radiation therapy through drinking water,they enter into the bodies of human beings and get accumulated there.

They cause various types of diseases. Mutation, birth defects, mental retardation, genetic disease cancer(breast,boneskin,etc),burn, cataracts, male sterility,Leukemia etc.

Effect of water pollution
1. Effects on Human health:-
The polluted water usually contains different pathogens such as virus, bacteria, parasites, protozoa and worms, therefore it is a source of water borne disease like cholera, typhoid, diarrhoea, dysentery, jaundice etc. Water contaminated with different heavy metals cause several diseases:-
Excessive mercury- Minamata disease in Japan
Cadmium poisoning lead to Itai-Itai disease in Japan also called Ouch-ouch disease (a painful disease of bones and joint) and cancers of lungs and liver.
Arsenic –cause Black Foot disease
Fluoride –Fluorosis.
Ground water pollution effect
Presence of excess nitrate (NO_3) in drinking water is dangerous for human health and may be fatal for infants.

Excess Nitrate in drinking water reacts with haemoglobin to form non-functional methaemoglonbin, and impairs oxygen transport.This condition is called methaemoglobinemia/ Blue Baby Syndrome.

Fluoride: Excess fluoride in drinking water causes neuro-muscular disorders, gastro-intestinal problems, teeth deformity, hardening of bones and stiff and painful joints(Skeletal Fluorosis).

High concentration of Fluoride ions is present in 13 states of India. According Indian Standards of drinking water, The maximum level of fluoride,which human body can tolerate is 1.5 mg/L of water. Long term ingestion of fluoride ions cause fluorosis.

Arsenic –Seepage of industrial and mine discharges, fly ash ponds of thermal power plants can lead to arsenic in ground water. In India and Bangladesh (Ganges Delta), millions of people are exposed to groundwater contaminated with high levels of arsenic, a highly toxic and dangerous pollutant. Chronic exposure to arsenic causes black foot disease. It also causes diarrhoea and also lung and skin cancer.

2.Effect on aquatic animals:-

Polluted water reduces Dissolved oxygen (DO) content thereby, eliminates sensitive organisms like fishes, planktons and other aquatic animals.

Hot water discharged from industries, when added to water bodies, lower its DO content.

3.Effect on food chains:

Water pollution disrupts the natural food chain. Metal pollutants such as lead and cadmium are eaten by small animals. Later on these animals are consumed by fish and shellfish,and the food chain continues to be interrupted at all higher levels.

Prevention and control of water pollution

Water pollutions can be controlled if everyone including governments and local councils get involved with. The following measures can be adopted in order to control water pollutants:

1.Proper dumping of waste:

Toxic products like paints, polished automobiles oil, and cleaning products should be stored and disposed of as far as possible. In fact, it is better to use non-toxic products as far as possible. Non-Biodegradable products like sanitary napkins, tampons, and diapers should not be flushed down in the toilets as these can damage the process of sewage treatment. The local authorities can visualize a chemical disposal plan for local residents.

2. Treatment of sewage water and industrial effluents should be done before releasing in into water bodies.

3. Hot water should be cooled before release from the power plants

4. Domestic cleaning in tanks, streams and rivers supply drinking water, should be prohibited

5. Excessive use of fertilizers and pesticides should be stopped.

6.People should be educated and government should start awareness about the water pollution.

7.Plant more tree

8. Government should start different schemes to grass roots levels for regulation and monitoring for the management of water pollution.

3.4.Soil Pollution

Soil pollution is defined as the contamination of soil by human and natural activities which may cause harmful effect on living organisms and the environment.

Causes of soil pollution
Soil pollution is mainly caused due to the following
1.Industrial wastes: The disposal of industrial wastes is the main problem for soil pollution.
It includes fly ash, chemical residues, metallic and nuclear wastes, industries chemicals, dyes and acids, etc.
2.Urban wastes: Urban waste comprises of both commercial and domestic wastes consisting of dried sludge and sewage. This consists of garbage and rubbish materials like plastics, glasses, metallic cans, fibres, paper, rubbers, street sweepings, fuel residues, leaves, products.
3.**Agricultural practices:** with the advance in agro-technology, vast quantities of fertilizers, pesticides, herbicides and weedicides are added to increase the crop yield. Fertilizers in the run off water these fields can cause eutrophication in water bodies. Pesticides are highly toxic chemicals which affect humans and other animals adversely causing respiratory problems, cancer and death. Apart from these, farm waste, manure, slurry debris, soil erosion containing mostly inorganic chemicals also cause soil pollution.
4.Radioactive pollutants:
Radioactives substances resulting from explosions of nuclear testing laboratories and industries giving rise to nuclear dust radioactive wastes which penetrate the soil and accumulate giving rise to soil pollution.
Example: Radio nuclides of Radium, Thorium, Uranium, Isotopes of Potassium(K-40) and Carbon(C-14) are usually found in soil, rock, water and air.
5. Biological Agents:

Soil gets a large amount of human, animals and bird execreta which constitute a major source of soil pollution by biological agents. **Example**, Heavy application of manures and digested sludge can cause serious damage to plants.

Effects of soil pollution

Soil pollution adversely affects human health, ecosystem, agriculture etc.

1.Effect on human health: The polluted soil affects human health through direct contact with soil or through inhalation of soil contaminants which have vaporized. The larger threats are posed by the infiltration of soil contamination into groundwater aquifers used for human consumption. Depending upon the pollutant type, way of attack and susceptibility of the exposed population, health consequences vary greatly from exposure to soil pollution.

2.Efect on ecosystem:

The chemistry of soil changes due to the presence of many hazardous chemicals in soil even at low concentration of the contaminant species. These changes can be apparent in the alteration of metabolism of microorganisms resident in a given soil environment. The result can be implicit suppression of some of the primary food chain, which in turn could have major consequences for predator or consumer species. Even if the chemical effect on lower life, the lower pyramid levels of the food chain may ingest foreign chemicals, which usually become more concentrated for each consuming step of the food chain.

3. Effect on agriculture

The contaminated soil is no longer be used to grow food, because the chemicals can leech into the food chain and harm people who eat it. If contaminated soil is used to grow food, the land will typically produce lower yields than it would if it were not contaminated. Consecutively, this can cause even more harm because lack of plants on the soil will cause more erosion, spreading the contaminants into soil that might not have been contaminated before contaminates normally alter plant metabolism which cause a reduction in crop yields and soil fertility.

Prevention and control of soil pollution

To control soil pollution, several measures can be undertaken and are as follows:

1.Reforesting: Trees and grass should be grown to check soil erosion.

2.Use of natural fertilizers: Application of organic manures and pesticides should be encouraged in agriculture.

3.Banning toxic chemicals: Industries should be banned from dumping toxic chemicals on agricultural land and proper disposal methods should be used.

4.Proper discarding of waste (unwanted materials)/Recycling and reuse of waste: Solid waste from urban and industrial areas should be disposed of using proper techniques and recycling.

5.Public awareness: Public awareness campaigns should be organized.

6. Government should provide subsidies, concessions and tax exemption to companies that use recycled raw materials.

3.5.Noise Pollution

Noise is defined as unwanted sound which is unpleasant to the ear. The word noise is defined as, "a loud, unpleasant or unwanted sound that causes discomfort to ears".

Noise pollution may be also defined as, "The unwanted sound dumped into the atmosphere leading to health hazards".

Noise pollution is loud disturbing dumped into ambient atmosphere without carrying for the adverse effect it may have.

It is a physical form of pollution that affects the receiver directly Sound is measured by decibels (dB).

A person hearing can be damaged if exposed to noise levels over 75Db over a prolonged period of time.

The WHO recommends that the sound level indoors should be less than 30dB

World Health Organization) has prescribed optimum noise level as 45 dB by day and 35 dB by night. Anything above 80 dB is hazardous

Noise becomes uncomfortable above 100 dB.

The Air (Prevention and Control of Pollution) Act 1981 was enacted for the control of air pollution, the problem of noise was also covered within the definition of air pollutants

Ambient Noise Level Monitoring

Noise Pollution (Control and Regulation) Rules, 2000 define ambient noise levels for various areas.

The Government of India on Mar 2011 launched a Real-time Ambient Noise Monitoring Network. Silence Zone is an area comprising not less than 100 metres around hospitals, educational institutions, courts, religious places or any other area declared as such by a competent authority.

Noise pollution (Control and Regulation) Rules, 2000 defined ambient noise levels for various areas as follows:-
Permissible Limit of Noise

Categories of Area/Zone	Day time(dB) 6.am- 10 pm	Night time(dB) 10pm to 6 am
Industrial area	75	70
Commercial area	65	55
Residential area	55	45
Silence zone	50	40

Under *Central Motor Vehicle Rule 1989*, the following were imposed on 26ᵗʰ March 1993

Types of vehicle	Limit of dB
Two wheelers(petrol run)	80 dB
Passenger car,petrol runs three wheelers,diesel run two wheelers	82 dB

	85 dB
Passenger or commercial vehicle upto 4MT	
Passenger/commercial vehicle above 4MT-12 MT	89
Passenger/commercial vehicles exceeding 12 MT	91

Sources of Noise Pollution

1. Industrial sources

The industrial sources may include noises from various industrial operating in cities like transportation, vehicular movement such as car, motor, truck, train, tempo, motor cycle, aircraft, rockets, defence, explosive etc.

2. Non-Industrial Sources:-

1. Loudspeakers

2. Construction works

3. Rood traffic

4. Trains

5. Agricultural machine

6. Religious and family ceremonies

7.Army practices like practice firing, rocket launches, explosions, jet trainings, tanks, etc.

8. Entertaining sources as radios, TVs, transistors, DVDs, CDs, computers, record players, other musical instruments, etc.

Causes of Noise Pollution

Industrialization: Most of the industries use big machines which are capable of producing large amount of noise. Apart from that, various equipments like compressors, generators, exhaust fans also contribute in producing big noise. Therefore, workers in these factories and industries wear ear plugs to minimize the effects of noise. Textile mills, printing presses, engineering establishments and metal works add heavily towards noise pollution

Poor urban Planning: In most of the developing countries, poor urban planning also plays a vital role in contributing to noise pollution. Congested houses, large families sharing small space, fight over parking and frequent fights over basic amenities leads to noise pollution which may disrupt the environment of society.

Social Events: Noise is at its peak in most of the social events. whether it is marriage, parties, pub, disc or place of worship, people normally break rules set by the local administration and create nuisance in the area. People play songs on full volume and dance till midnight which makes the condition of people living nearby. In markets, people selling clothes via making loud noise to attract the attention of people also add to noise pollution.

Transportation: Large number of vehicles on road, Aeroplan's flying over houses, trains proved to be a big source of noise pollution. Increasing traffic has given rise to traffic jams in congested areas where the repetitive hotting of horns by impatient drivers pierces the ears of all road users.

Construction activities: construction activities like mining, bridges, dams, building, roads, flyovers.

Household chores: Domestic gadget like TV, Mobile, mixer grinder, pressure cooker, vacuum cleaners, washing machine and dryer, cooler, air conditioners etc., are minor contributors to the quantity of noise pollution.

Effects of Noise Pollution

Noise effect is categorically, performance, physiology and psychology.

It cause hearing problems, sleeping problems, cardiovascular issues, trouble in communication

a. Various Psychological effect of noise pollution are

1. Noise pollution cause anxiety and stress
2. Depression and fatigue, which considerably reduces the efficiency of a person.

3. **Annoyance:** Noise, which is an annoyance also causes irritation dis-satisfaction, dis-interest and affects work performance.
4. **Sleeplessness:** It affects the sleep of people become restless and loses concentration and presence of mind during their activities.
5. **Nervous system:** It causes pain, ringing in the ears, feelings of tiredness, thereby effecting the functioning of human system.

b. Various Physiological effects of noise pollution are as under:-
1. Noise pollution affects human health, comfort and efficiency. It causes contraction of blood vessels, makes the skin pale, and leads to excessive secretion of adrenalin hormone into blood stream.
2. **Loss of hearing**: long exposure of high sound levels cause loss of hearing. This is mostly unnoticed but has an adverse impact on hearing function.
3. Psychological effects of noise pollution include neurosis, hypertension, increase in sweating hepatic disease, change in intestinal activities behavioural and emotional stress.
4. Noise mainly interfere with man's communication.
5. Blood gets thickened by excessive noise.
6. Noise can cause chronic headache and irritability, work, which needs a high degree of skill is considerably affected.
7. Deafness may be caused due to permanent damage of sensory cells of hearing when subjected to prolonged and continued exposure of noise. Temporary deafness occurs at 4000-6000 Hz and beyond 100 dB.

c. Human Performance effect of noise pollution:-
The working performance of human. Workers will be affected as it distracts the concentration.

d.Other damage:-Damage of material: Excessive noise can also cause buildings and materials may get damaged by exposure of infrasonic/ultrasonic waves and even get collapsed.

Prevention and control of noise pollution

1. Highway traffic should not be allowed to pass through towns and cities. It should be diverted through bye-passes and over-bridges. Pressure horns should not be allowed.
2. Prohibition on usage of loud speaker.
3. Noisy machines should be installed in sound-proof chambers.
4. Proper lubrication and maintenance of machines and automobile can reduce noise.
5. Protective devices like ear muffs or cotton plugs should be provided to workers working in noisy installations.
6. Green belt development (planting of trees)
7. 4-5 rows of trees and shrubs should be grown along roads, rails, around industrial area and residential complexes in order to decrease the intensity of the sound. These rows of trees are also called as Green Belts. They reduce noise level by 10-15 dB. Trees help reduce noise pollution by absorbing sound. Example: Neem, Ashoka, Tamarind, etc.
8. Enforcing acoustic zoning by keeping human settlements away from noise producing industries, aerodromes, railway stations etc. Silence zones should be created for educational institutes, hospitals and important offices.
9. Control over vibration

Legislative measures taken

Excessive noise has been registered as a crime (Section 268 of IPC).

Noise Pollution (Regulation and Control) Rules, 2000 have been notified.

Noise has been recognized as a pollutant (Environment Act 1986).

Day and night limits of noise level have been prescribed.

100 metre radius area around hospitals, educational institutions and courts has been declared a 'Silence Zone' where use of horns, loudspeakers and bursting of crackers is banned.

Use of loudspeakers is a public nuisance and is punishable under section 133 of IPC.

There are provisions related to noise pollution under Motor Vehicle Act, Factories Act, Railways Act and Aircraft Act.

3.6. Constitutional provisions for environmental protection in India

The awareness and consideration for environment covers several environmental issues such as pollution of water, air and soil, land degradation, industrialization, urbanization, depletion of natural resources etc.

Legislation also serves as a valuable tool for educating masses about their responsibility in maintaining healthy environment

6.1. Environmental Law
Environmental Law

As an instrument to protect and improve the environment and control or prevent any act or omission polluting or likely to pollute the environment"

Legislation also serves as a valuable tool for educating masses about their responsibility in maintaining healthy environment.

Numerous legislations have already been put forth at national and international levels.

Indian legislations are **called Acts** whereas the international legislations are in the form of **conventions, protocols and treaties.**

6.2. Earlier Environmental Legislation in India.

India has a long history of environmentalism and there was various enactment to check the environmental issues in the country.

 Some of the important acts framed were

a. Indian Panel code 1860

b.   Madras Wild Elephant Preservation Act,1873
c.   All India Elephant Preservation Act,1879
d.   Wild Birds and Animals Preservation Acts. 1912
e.   Bengal Rhinoceros Preservation Acts 1932
f.   Assam Rhinoceros Preservation Acts, 1972
g.   Indian Wild-Life (Protection) Act, 1972.
h.   Factories Act 1948
i.   The mine and minerals(Development and regulation)Act, 1952

2.Legislation restricting hunting, killing or over-exploitation of a species

In India, the earliest laws made in this connection concerned wild Elephants, which were enacted as early as 1873 A.D and 1879 A.D, following which a number of wild animals attracted states' attention.

3. Legislation for the Protection of Wild-Life.

Some of the acts promulgated were:-

1.Bengal Smoke Nuisance Act, 1905

2.Indian Ports Acts,1907

3. The Motor Vehicle Act, 1939.

However, in the post-independence India, due to rapid changes and non-effective implementation, these provisions were ineffective in checking environmental degradation.

6.3.National Legislation

At national level serious efforts have been made for the improvement and protection of environment by incorporating changes the constitution of India.

Our Indian constitution, originally, did not contain any direct provision regarding the protection of natural environment. **However, after the United Nations Conference on Human Environment, held in Stockholm in 1972.**

Indian constitution was amended to include protection of the

environment as a constitutional mandate. India was the first

country to amend the constitution of India endorsing

environmental protection and improvement.

Constitutional provisions
India was the first country to amend the constitution of India endorsing environmental protection and improvement.
The 42nd Amendment Act was adopted in 1976 and came to effect in January,1977.
DPSP mentioned in articles 47 added a new dimension by obliging the central government to protect environment.
Fundamental Rights
The Hon'ble SC in several cases interpreted the right of life and personal liberty to include the right to a whole environment.
Article 21: Right to clean environment is guaranteed in Indian constitution.
The Law of Torts on Public and Private Nuisance
A polluter may also be liable in Tort for causing private and public nuisance. Sending deleterious substance like gas, smoke or filth on the property of another person is private nuisance. A civil action can also lie for public nuisance in that circumstance in which a criminal action U/S 268 of IPC can be taken.
The 'Right to Life' contained in Article-21 of the Constitution of India includes the **right to clean and human environment.** It means you have the right to live in a clean and healthy environment.

DPSP articles 47 and Article 48A:
Article-38 of our Constitution requires State to ensure a social order for the welfare of people, which can be obtained by an unpolluted and clean environment only
Article 47 : It defines duties of states of raise the level of nutrients and the standards of living and to improve public health
Articles 48A:-Directive Principle of state policy statement:
"The state shall endeavor to protect and improve the environment and to safeguard the forest and wildlife of the country"
Article-48A of the Constitution requires the State to adopt the Protectionist policy as well as Improvinistic Policy.
 Protectionist policy imposes ban on those things which lead to environmental degradation, e.g.ban on use of leaded petrol, ban on

use of plastic bags etc.

Improvinistic policy refers to alternatives that can be used for improvement of environment, e.g. use of CNG or low sulphur fuel, tree plantation in industrial areas etc.

Added in 1976, the 42 Constitutional Amendment.

Ractifies the Stockholm Conference on 1972.

Article 48-A was inserted under the Directive Principles of State Policy(DPSP).

Article 51A (g)

Article 51A constitutes the fundamental Duties of a citizen.

This point (g) in Art.51A reads

"It shall be the duty of every citizen of India to protect and improve the natural environment including forest, lakes, rivers, and wildlife and to have compassion for living creatures"

Articles 51A(g) was inserted as one of the Fundamental Duties.

Most of the Acts and laws then are based on this articles.

Environmental Protection Act 1986 is the instrument of executive.

There are a number of laws to protect India's environment in the jurisdiction of the federal and state governments

Article 253 of the constitution empowers parliaments to make laws relating to international agreements and conventions and harmonize national legislation with the international agreements and conventions.

However, the constitution has no provision empowering the central government to enact domestic laws pertaining to environmental issues applied uniformity to all the states.

Some Items of environment legislation are in the state list and the central government has to approach the state for it.

For example water is on the state list and Article 252 mentions that at least two or more state legislatures should pass resolution empowering the parliament to pass water related laws.

Ministry of Health introduced the Prevention of Water Pollution Bill in 1969 after a lot of deliberations. The modified versions, the Water(Prevention and Control of Pollution) was passed in 1974.Thereafter, the Air(Prevention and Control of Pollution) Act was enacted in 1981.The task of implementation of this legislation was entrusted to the same regulatory agency created under the Water (Prevention and Control)Act,1974.

The Stockholm Conference on Human Environment,1972 emphasized a need to adopt comprehensive legislation for environmental problems endangering health and safety of people and flora and fauna. A national committee on Environmental Planning and coordination(NCEPC) was set up with an objective to deal with issues like appraisal of development projects, human settlement planning, survey of ecosystems, like wetland and spread environmental education.

In 1980, Government of India appointed Tiwari Committee on environmental issues. On its recommendation, Department of Environment (DOE) was established on November 1,1980 as a nodal agency for environmental project, pollution monitoring and regulation, monitoring of air and water quality and coordinated between local, state and central governments. However, it served as an advisory body without enforcement powers.

In 1985, Prime Minister Rajiv Gandhi, with an objective to overcome short comings created Ministry of Environment and Forest (MoEF) comprising of 28 divisions and two independent units holding prime importance, Ganga project Directorate and National Mission on Wastelands Developments. It furthered the works originally with DOE, viz., monitoring and enforecement, conducting environmental assessments and surveys, undertaking promotional works etc.

In 1986,the Parliament enacted a comprehensive legislation in Environment,the Environmental (Protection) Act 1986.The task to administer the new legislation was entrusted to the central and state pollution control boards. Then laws addressing specific environmental problems were passed like, The Wildlife Protection Act, The Atomic Energy Act etc. MoEF completed its Environmental Action Plan in December,1993 to integrate environmental considerations and developments plans. It employed a number of strategies like, implementation of polluter pays principle, water cess, water consumption charges with additional charge for excessive water use, technical assistance to promote central effluent treatment plants etc. and pursued pollution abatement and prevention policy.

3.7. The Wildlife Protection Act ,1972

The most significant legislation on wildlife protection which is based on the ecosystem approach and a regulatory regime of command and control is the **Wild Life Protection Act, 1972.**

The objective of this enactment was three-fold...

1. To have a uniform legislation on wild life throughout the country
2. To establish a network of protected areas, i. e., national parks and sanctuaries
3. To regulate illicit trade in wild life and its products.

History behind WLP Act, 1972

The earliest codified law can be traced to 3rd Centaury B.C. when Ashoka, the King of Maghadha, enacted a law in the matter of preservation of wild life and environment.

But, the first codified law in India which heralded the era of laws for the wild life and protection was enacted in the year 1887 by the British and was titled as the Wild Birds Protection Act, 1887 (10 of 1887).

This Act enabled the then Government to frame rules prohibiting the possession or sale of any kinds of specified wild birds, which have been killed or taken during the breeding season.

Again the British Government in the year 1912 passed the Wild Birds and Animals Protection Act, 1912 (8 of 1912) as the Act of 1887 proved to be inadequate for the protection of wild birds and animals.

The Act of 1912 was amended in the year 1935 by the Wild Birds and Animals Protection (Amendment) Act, 1935 (27 of 1935)

After the Second World War the freedom struggle for India started taking its shape and wild life was relegated to the background.

But after independence, the Constituent Assembly in the Draft Constitution placed "Protection of Wild Birds and Wild Animals" at entry No.20 in the State List and the State Legislature has been given power to legislate.

It was not till late 1960's that the concern for the depleting wild finally aroused.

The first comprehensive legislation relating to protection of wild life was passed by the Parliament and it was assented by the President on **9th September, 1972** and came to be known as The Wild Life (Protection) Act, 1972.

Wildlife Protection Act 1972

The Indian Parliament enacted the Wildlife (Protection) Act in 1972, which provides for the safeguard and protection of the wildlife (flora and fauna) in the country.

This Act provides for the protection of the country's wild animals, birds and plant species, in order to ensure environmental and ecological security. Among other things, the Act lays down restrictions on hunting many animal species.

An amendment to the Act in 1982, introduced a provision permitting the capture and Transportation of wild animals for the scientific management of animal population

This act was amended subsequently in 1986,1991 and 1993 to accommodate provision for its effective implementation.

The Act was last amended in the year 2006. An Amendment bill was introduced in the Rajya Sabha in 2013 and referred to a Standing Committee, but it was withdrawn in 2015.

Constitutional Provisions for the Wildlife Act

Article 48A of the Constitution of India directs the State to protect and improve the environment and the safeguard wildlife and forests. This article was added to the Constitution by the 42nd Amendment in 1976.

Article 51A imposes certain fundamental duties for the people of India. One of them is to protect and improve the natural environment including forests, lakes, rivers and wildlife and to have compassion for living creatures.

3.8.The Water (prevention and Control of Pollution) Cess Act 1977

The Water Cess Act was passed to generate financial resources to meet expenses of the **Central and State Pollution Boards.**

The Act creates economic incentives for pollution control and requires local authorities and certain designated industries to pay a cess for water effluent discharge.

These revenues are used to implement the Water Act.

The Central Government, after deducting the expenses of collection, pays the central board and the states such sums, as it seems necessary.

To encourage capital investment in pollution control, the Act gives a polluter a 70% rebate of the applicable cess upon installing effluent treatment equipment

3.9.Forest (Conservation)Act, 1980, Amended in 1988.

First Forests Act was enacted in 1927, which provided-Reserved Forest, protected forests and Village Forest .

This act is not applicable to J &K

Alarmed at India's rapid deforestation and resulting environmental degradation, the Parliament has enacted the **Forest (Conservation) Act, 1980**, to check further deforestation and conserve forests and to provide for matters connected therewith or ancillary or incidental thereto.

Salient Features of Forests Conservation Act 1980

This Act has five Sections which deal with conservation of forests.

The Act was enacted with the twin objectives under Section 2 of restricting the use of forest land for non-forest purposes, and preventing the de-reservation of forests that have been reserved under the Indian Forest Act, 1927. However, in 1988 the Act was further amended to include two new provisions under Section 2, where it sought to restrict leasing of forest land to private individuals, authority, corporations not owned by the Government, and to prevent clear felling of naturally grown trees.

It was enacted to consolidate the law related to forest, the transit of forest produces and the duty liveable on timber and other forest produce.

Forest officers and their staff administer the Forest Act.Under the provisions of this Act, **prior approval of the Central Government** is required for diversion of forestlands for non-forest purposes.

No diversion for cultivation or any other purpose other than aforestation. But restriction does not include development and management of forest and wildlife. Establishment of check post, firelines wireless communication, bridges, boundary marks etc.

Diversion of forest land is also allowed to meet the developmental needs for Drinking water projects, Irrigation projects, Transmission lines, Railways lines, Roads, Power project, Defense related project, Mining etc. Such diversions of forest land for non-forestry purposes, compensatory afforestation is stipulated to mitigate the ill effects of diversion of such vast area of green forests.

An Advisory Committee constituted under the Act advises the Centre on these approvals.

The Act deals with the four categories of the forests, namely reserved forests, village forests, protected forests and private forests.

Reserved forest

A state may declare forestlands or waste lands as reserved forest and may sell the produce from these forests.

Any unauthorized felling of trees quarrying, grazing and hunting in reserved forests is punishable with a fine or imprisonment, or both.

Village forests

Reserved forests assigned to a village community are called village forests.

Protected forests

The **state governments are empowered to designate protected forests** and may prohibit the felling of trees, quarrying and the removal of forest produce from these forests.

The preservation of protected forests is enforced through rules, licenses and criminal prosecutions.

3.10. National Forest Policy 1988

India is one of the few countries which has a Forest Policy since **1894. Revised in 1952**, the policy was revised in 1988, and Came to be known as the **National Forest Policy 1988.**

According to the new forest policy, the Government will emphasizes sustainable forest management in order to protect, conserve and expand forest reserve and to meet the needs of local people on the other.

Salient Features and Goals of National Forest Policy-

1. Bringing 33 percent of the geographical areas under forest cover;
2. Maintenance of environmental stability through preservation and restoration of ecological balance
3. Conservation of Natural Heritage(existing) of the country, its biological diversity and genetic pool
4. Checking Soil Erosion, Checking extension of sand dunes in desert lands and reduction of floods and droughts.
5. Substantially increasing Forest/Tree Cover through Afforestation and Social Forestry on degraded land.
6. Increasing the productivity of forests to meet requirements of fuel, wood, fodder, minor forest produces, soil and timber of Rural and Tribal Population.
7. Increasing the productivity of Forests to meet National Needs.
8. Encouraging efficient utilization of Forest Produce and Optimum Use of Wood(Timber)
9. Generation of Work Opportunities, the involvement of Women.
10. Creating of a massive people's movement involving women to encourage planting of trees, stop deforestation and thus, reduce pressure on the existing forest.

Major Achievement of National Forest Policy 1988

1. Increase in the forest and tree cover
2. Involvement of local communities in the protection, conservation and management of forests through joint forest Management Programme.
3. Meeting the requirement of fuel woods, fodder minor forest products and small timber of the rural and tribal populations.
4. Conservation of Biological Diversity and Genetic Resources of the country through ex-situ and In-situ conservation measures.

5. Significant contribution in maintenance of environment and ecological stability in the country

Shortcoming of the NFP 1988

No Official definition of the term "Forest", which may comprise of a "Self-Sown" area which supports a Community of Creatures dependant on the plants and Interdependent on each other.

"Natural Heritage" should include All Green Cover such as Grasslands, Wetlands and Other Ecosystems.

No provision for protection of Degraded Land which if Protected may be productive in the Future.

It does not focus on methods to check soil-erosion, denudation, Floods, etc

The principal Aim should be to ensure a Healthy Natural Environment and Maintenance of Healthy Functioning of Life Support Systems.

A Draft National Forest Policy was updated on the website of Ministry of Environment, Forests and Climate Change on June, 2016, the Forest Policy, 2016 was repealed. The ministry of environment, forest and climate change has framed a new draft National Forest Policy 2018 which proposes climate change mitigation through sustainable forest management.

3.11. The Air (Prevention and Control of Pollution) Act 1981 and amended 1987

To implement the decisions taken at the United Nations Conference on the Human Environment held at Stockholm in June 1972, Parliament enacted the nationwide Air Act.

The Air (Prevention and Control of Pollution) Act, 1981 extends to the whole of India.

"**Air pollutant**" means any solid, liquid or gaseous substance 2[(including noise)] present in the atmosphere in such concentration as may be or tend to be injurious to human beings or other living creatures or plants or property or environment;

"**Air pollution,**" means the presence in the atmosphere of any air pollutants.

Salient Features

Important provisions of this Act are given below:

The main objectives of this Act are to improve the quality of air and to prevent, control and abate air pollution in the country.

The Air Act's framework is similar to that of the Water Act of 1974. To enable an integrated approach to environmental problems, the Air Act expanded the authority of the central and state boards established under the Water Act, to include air pollution control.

States not having water pollution boards were required to set up air pollution boards.

Under the Air Act, all industries operating within designated air pollution control areas must obtain a "consent" (permit) from the State Boards.

The states board are required to prescribe emission standards for industry and automobiles after consulting the central board and noting its ambient air quality standards.

1987 Amendment empowered the board to close down a defaulting industries or may stop its supply of electricity or water.

Salient features of this Act

The major sections and features of this Act are-

Section 3- The Central and State Pollution Control Boards have the responsibility to exercise the powers provided under this Act without prejudice.

Section 4- In states where there is a Water Pollution Control Board established, the same shall be given the joint responsibility of controlling and monitoring air pollution, and will be called State Pollution Control Board.

Section 5- In states where there is no Water Pollution Control Board, a new Pollution Control Board will be set up.

Section 16 describes the functions of the Central Pollution Control Board, some of which includes-

Advice the Central government on matters pertaining to air and air pollution.

Advice and support State Boards in carrying out their functions.

Carry out research related to air pollution.

Through mass media, spread awareness and information about air and air pollution.

Plan and organize the training of personnel.

Set the standards for Air Quality in India.

Section 17 describes the functions of the State Pollution Control, some of which are-

Advice the State Government on matters of air and air pollution.

In collaboration with the Central Board, plan and organize the training of personnel.

Carry out inspections in air pollution control areas at necessary intervals.

Advice the State Government about the feasibility of conducting industrial activity with respect to air pollution.

Section 19- The SPCBs have the authority to declare any area as an air pollution control area, with consultation from the CPCB.

Section 21 states that no person or entity shall establish an industry without prior permission from the Boards in an air pollution control area.

Section 22 states that no person or industry shall emit air pollutants above the standards set by the Pollution Control Boards. Under section 22A, the Board can even approach a court to gain a restraining order on the industry/persons from causing air pollution.

Section 26 gives **any officer of the Pollution Control Boards,, the power to take samples from any chimney, duct, etc. for testing** and seeing whether the emissions are within prescribed standards or not.

Section 28- This allows the SPCBs to set up State Air Laboratories, either as a new establishment or by declaring an existing lab as a State Air Lab. These labs have the authority to test the air samples and air quality procedures as described by the standards, for the SPCBs of that state in their areas.

Section 37, the law states that **failure to comply with the rules of Section 21 and 22 will result in punishment that is a minimum of one year and 6 months, but extendable up to 6 years with fine**. If the failure continues, an additional fine of 25,000 rupees per day is introduced till the time the offence does not stop. If the failure continues for more than a year, then the culprit is punishable by imprisonment for a minimum of 2 years and can extend up to 7 years with fine.

3.12.Environmental (Protection) Act 1986

Enact on March 1986 and Came into force 19ᵗʰ Nov 1986 under **Article 253**.It has 26 sections and 4 chapters.

In the wake of the Bhopal tragedy, the government of India enacted the Environment (Protection) Act of 1986. The purpose of the Act is to implement the decisions of the United Nations Conference on the Human Environment of 1972.The genesis of the Environmental (Protection) Act 1986 is the more effective and bolt measures to fight the problem of pollution.The genesis of the environmental (Protection)Act 1986 is in the Article 48A of Directive Principle of State Policy and Articles 51A(g) of the Fundamental Duties of the Indian ConstitutionThe Act is an "umbrella" for legislations designed to provide a framework for Central Government, coordination of the activities of various central and state authorities established under previous Acts, such as the Water Act and the Air Act.In this Act, main emphasis is given to "Environment", defined to include water, air and land and the inter-relationships which exist among water, air and land and human beings and other living creatures, plants, micro-organisms and property.

"Environmental pollution" is the presence of pollutant, defined as any solid, liquid or gaseous substance present in such a concentration as may be or may tend to be injurious to the environment.**"Hazardous substances"** include any substance or preparation, which may cause harm to Human beings, other living creatures, plants, microorganisms, property or the environment.

Main objectives of The Environment (Protection) Act 1986

1. The main aim is to provide for the protection and improvement of environment.
2. To the protection and improvement of the human environment and the prevention of hazards to human beings, other living creatures, plants and property.
3. The standards of quality of air, water and soil for various area and purpose.
4. The procedures and safeguards for the handling of hazardous substances in different areas.
5. The prohibition and restriction on the location of industries and to carry on process and operations in different areas

Salient features of Environmental (Protection) Act 1986
The main provisions of this Act are given below
Section 3 (1) of the Act empowers the center to "take all such measures as it deems necessary or expedient for the purpose of protecting and improving the quality of the environment and preventing, controlling and abating environmental pollution".

Specifically, the Central Government is authorized to set new national standards for the quality of the environment (ambient standards) as well as standards for controlling emissions and effluent discharges; to regulate industrial locations, to prescribe procedures for managing hazardous substances; to establish safeguards preventing accidents, and to collect and dismantle information regarding environmental pollution.

By virtue of this Act, Central Government has armed itself with considerable powers which include, coordination of action by state, planning and execution of nation wide programmes, laying down environmental quality standards, especially those governing emission or discharge of environmental pollutants, placing restriction on the location of industries and so on.

The coverage of powers includes handling of hazardous substances, prevention of environmental accidents, inspection of polluting units, research, establishment of laboratories, dissemination of information, etc.

The Environment (Protection) Act was the first environmental legislation to give the Central Government authority to issue direct orders, included orders to close, prohibit or regulate any industry, operation or process or to stop or regulate the supply of electricity, water or any other service to an industry, operation and process. Another power granted to the Central Government was to ensure compliance with the Act which included the power of entry for examination, testing of equipment and other purposes and power to analyze the sample of air, water, soil or any other substance from any place.

The Act explicitly prohibits discharges of environmental pollutants in excess of prescribed regulatory standards. There is also a specific prohibition against handling hazardous substances except those in compliance with regulatory procedures and standards. Persons responsible for discharge of pollutants in excess of prescribed standards must prevent or mitigate the pollution and must also to report the governmental authorities.

The Act provides provision for penalties. Any person who fails to comply with any of the provisions of the Act, or the rules, orders, or directions issued under the Act shall be punished. For each failure or contravention the punishment included a prison term up to five years or fine up to Rs. 1 lakh, or both. The Act imposed an additional fine of up to Rs. 5,000 for every day of continuing violation. If a failure or contravention, Occurs for more than one year after the date of conviction, an offender may punished with imprisonment term, which may be extend to seven years

The Environment (Protection) Act 1986 contains significant innovations for its enforcement, not contained in any other pollution control legislation at the time of the Act's adoption.

Section 19 provides that any person, in addition to authorized government officials, may file a complaint with a court alleging an offence under the Act. This "Citizens' Suit" provision requires that the person has to give notice of not less than 60 days of the alleged offence of pollution to the Central Government or the competent authority. Under the Act, the Central Government may, by notification in the office Gazette, make rules for the enforcement of the Act.

3.13. Scheduled Tribes and other Traditional Forest Dwellers(Recognition of Forest Rights) Act,2006

Scheduled Tribes and Other Traditional Forest Dwellers(Recognition of Forest Rights) Act,2006 recognizes the forest rights and vests the occupation of forestland in the Scheduled Tribes and traditional dwellers who have continued to live in the forest for generations and yet their rights have remained unrecorded. This Acts recognizes the right to dwell on the lands of the forests. It recognizes that such a land can be under individual or common occupation either for the habitation or self-cultivation for one's livelihood.

Silent features of Schedule Tribes and other traditional forest dwellers Act 2006

The Scheduled Tribes and Other Traditional Forest Dwellers (Recognition of Forest Rights) Act, 2006, commonly known as the Forest Rights Act (FRA), is a significant legislation aimed at recognizing and securing the forest rights of tribal communities and other traditional forest dwellers in India. Here are some key features: **Recognition of Forest Rights**: The Act recognizes the rights of Scheduled Tribes and other traditional forest dwellers to hold and live in forest land under individual or common occupation for habitation or self-cultivation or livelihood.

Scope: It applies to all states except Jammu and Kashmir and covers both forestland and wasteland traditionally used by these communities.

Rights Granted: The Act provides for the granting of titles or rights to individuals and communities over forest land and resources they have been traditionally using. This includes rights such as ownership, access to collect and use minor forest produce, grazing rights, etc.

Recognition of Community Forest Rights: It recognizes the rights of communities to protect, regenerate, conserve, and manage any community forest resource which they have been traditionally protecting and conserving for sustainable use.

Procedure for Recognition of Rights: The Act lays down the process for filing claims and their verification. Gram Sabhas (village assemblies) play a crucial role in the identification of forest rights.

Conservation Measures: While recognizing the rights of forest dwellers, the Act also emphasizes the need for conservation and sustainable management of forests and wildlife.

Conflict Resolution: It establishes a mechanism for the resolution of disputes related to forest rights.

Empowerment of Forest Dwellers: The Act aims to empower forest-dwelling communities by giving them legal recognition and control over their traditional lands and resources.

The rights under this Act are granted only to those who dwell in the forest or depend on the forest or the forest land for earning their livelihood and the claimant should either belong to any Scheduled Tribe that are scheduled in the said area or should be dwelling on the forest land in the last 75 years.

Overall, the Forest Rights Act is a landmark legislation that seeks to correct historical injustices against forest-dwelling communities and promote their socio-economic development while ensuring the conservation of forests and wildlife.

3.14.International Environmental Legislation

Till today, there is no international legislation body in the world with authority to pass legislation similar to National Legislations, nor are there International Authority Agencies with power to regulate resources at a global scale.

As a result, international legislation must depend on the agreement of the parties concerned. Certain issues of multinational concern are addressed by collection of policies, agreements, protocols and treaties that are loosely **called International Environmental Legislations.**

Most of the international legislations are international agreements to which nations adhere voluntarily. These agreements are generally finalized through international conventions or treaties.

Nations that have agreed to be bound by the convention are known as Parties.

Treaties and Convention provides a framework to be respected by each party, which has to adopt its own national legislations to make sure that convention is implemented at national level.

To support the conventions, some time protocols are also to be framed.

A protocol is an international agreement that stands on its own but is linked to an existing convention. It means that the climate protocol shares the concerns and principles set out in the climate convention. It then builds on these by adding new commitments-which are stronger and far more complex and detailed than those in the convention.

The evolution of international environmental law has been shaped by increasing global awareness of environmental issues and the need for coordinated efforts to address them.
 The evolution of international environmental law can be categorized into three distinct periods: -
•from1900-1972,
•from1972-1994;
•and from 1992-todate.

3.15. The Evolution of International Environmental Law

The evolution of International Environmental Law (IEL) can be divided into distinct periods:
1. FROM 1900-1972:
2. FROM 1972-1992:
2. FROM 1992-2012 ,upto date

As early as 1900 just after the Berlin Conference 1884 when parts of Africa were distributed to colonial powers the first treaties with standards for regulating wildlife including flora and fauna through protected areas were initiated.
•1940s issues of navigation at sea, whaling and fishing brought in 4 treaties relating to the Law of the Sea.

The Stockholm Conference of 1972 was responding to the effects of the industrial revolution to address pollution.The outcome documents of the Stockholm Conference including the principles bring out clear concerns then for natural resources depletion and pollution related issues. UN Environment established to address these

Phase 1: From 1900-1972,

During this era, international environmental awareness was limited. Initiatives like the London Convention of 1900 aimed to protect African wildlife but failed to gain sufficient support.

As early as 1900 just after the Berlin Conference 1884 when parts of Africa were distributed to colonial powers the first treaties with standards for regulating wildlife including flora and fauna through protected areas were initiated.

1940s issues of navigation at sea, whaling and fishing brought in 4 treaties relating to the Law of the Sea

Notable developments include the establishment of the United Nations and the first UN Conference on the Human Environment in 1972, which produced the Stockholm Declaration, recognizing the right to a healthy environment and laying the foundation for IEL.

The Stockholm Conference of 1972 was responding to the effects of the industrial revolution to address pollution.

The outcome documents of the Stockholm Conference including the principles bring out clear concerns then for natural resources depletion and pollution related issues.

UN Environment established to address these.

Evolution
From 1900-1972,

Wildlife management;

Natural resource conservation –regulating use; Wetlands of International Importance; Marine resources, and navigation;

UN General Assembly Resolutions including resolution 1972 for establishing UNEP;

Phase 2.

This period saw significant changes in national governments, the creation of green political parties, and the formation of Ministries of Environment. In 1983, the World Commission on Environment and Development (the Brundtland Commission) was established.

In 1992, key conventions like the Convention on Biological Diversity and the United Nations Framework Convention on Climate Change were presented and the Rio Declaration reaffirmed the Stockholm Declaration's principles

Convention on International Trade in Endangered Species (CITES); Wetlands; Heritage; -1973
Law of the Sea (UNCLOS), 11 Regional Seas Conventions; International Maritime Organization (IMO) Conventions, MARPOL, Oil preparedness.
Stockholm Declaration with a set of global environmental principles;
Vienna Convention Protection of Ozone Layer & Montreal Protocol plus amendments (Kigali); Basel Convention;
1987 Our Common Future-Brundtland Report defining Sustainable Development
-Nairobi Declaration   1982
-Bonn Convention/CMS 1983
-Vienna Convention   1985
-Montreal Convention 1987
-Basal Convention   1989
-Kigali Pact   2016

From 1972-1992;
•Convention on International Trade in Endangered Species (CITES); Wetlands; Heritage;
•Law of the Sea (UNCLOS), 11 Regional Seas Conventions; International Maritime Organization (IMO) Conventions, MARPOL, Oil preparedness.
•Stockholm Declaration with a set of global environmental principles;
•Vienna Convention Protection of Ozone Layer & Montreal Protocol plus amendments (Kigali); Basel Convention;
•1987 Our Common Future- Brundtland Report defining Sustainable Development.
Sustainable Development:
The Brundtland report defined Sustainable Development as development that meets the needs of the present without compromising the future generation to meet their own needs.
• 1992 UN Environment and Development Conference;

- 2000 MDGs, CSD;
- 2002 World Summit on Sustainable Development 2012 UN Conference on Sustainable Development; SDG Conference, HLPF.

Phase 3. From 1992-2012 , upto date
United Nations Conference on Environment and Development, Rio de Janeiro, Brazil, 1992
Outcome-Agenda 21 implemented in all countries including local authorities;
Rio Declaration-with environment and development principles.
Rio Conventions-CBD, UNFCCC, Forest Principles, Desertification,
Stockholm on POPs
Rotterdam on PIC
SAICM
Minamata
UNCCD) United Nations Convention to Combat Desertification-1994
Global Tiger Forum 1993
United Nations Forum On Forest(UNFF) 2000
Bio safety (Cartagena Biosafety protocol 2000)
Paris agreement -2015
Marrakech Agreement -2016
Bonn(Germany) COP23-2017
Katowice(Poland) COP24 2018
SDGs targets, indicators.
IEL predominantly develops through dynamic environmental treaty systems, created and maintained by member states to govern specific aspects of international environmental relations.
This evolution reflects the growing global recognition of the need for coordinated efforts to address environmental challenges, making IEL a crucial field in contemporary international law.
Thus, the evolution of International Environmental Law, from its early beginnings to its contemporary significance in addressing global environmental issues.

15.1. United Nations Environment Programme(UNEP)

- ➢ UNEP is an **agency of the United Nations**.
- ➢ It **coordinates the UN's environmental activities**.
- ➢ It was founded as a result of the United Nations Conference on the Human Environment 1972.
- ➢ WMO & UNDP jointly established IPCC(1988).It has 195 members.
- ➢ It has overall responsibility for environmental problems among United Nations agencies.
- ➢ **UNEP** was set up in 1972 to serve as a catalyst in developing and coordinating an environmental focus in the programmes of other organisations.
- ➢ <u>**UNEP was establishing at HQ Nairobai, Kenya on 5th June 1972**</u> as an outcome of UN Conference on the Human Environment at Stockholm.
- ➢ UNEP also has six regional offices and various country offices.
- ➢ **The United Nations Environment Programme** (UN Environment) is the leading global environmental authority that sets the global environmental agenda, promotes the coherent implementation of the environmental dimension of sustainable development within the United Nations system, and serves as an authoritative advocate for the global environment. UNEP's work include;
1. Assessing global, regional and national environmental conditions and trends.
2. Developing International and National Environmental Instruments and.
3. Strengthening Institutions for the Wise Management of the environment.

Objective of UNEP

- ➢ To provide leadership and encourage partnership in caring for the environment by inspiring, informing, and enabling nations and peoples to improve their quality of life without compromising that of future generations.

Focus areas of UNEP

1. Climate change

2. Disasters and conflicts
3. Ecosystem management
4. Environmental governance
5. Chemicals and waste
6. Resource efficiency, and

Environment under review

UNEP has also been active in funding and implementing environment related development projects.

UNEP has aided in the formulation of guidelines and treaties on issues such as the international trade in potentially harmful chemicals, transboundary air pollution, and contamination of international waterways

UNEP is also one of several Implementing Agencies for the **Global Environment Facility (GEF)** and the Multilateral Fund for the Implementation of the **Montreal Protocol**

The International Cyanide Management Code, a program of best practice for the chemical's use at gold mining operations, was developed under UNEP's aegis

The **World Meteorological Organization** and **UN Environment** established the **Intergovernmental Panel on Climate Change (IPCC)** in 1988.

It is also a member of the **United Nations Development Group**.

UNEP has registered several successes, such as the **1987 Montreal Protocol**, and the **2013 Minamata Convention**, a **treaty to limit toxic mercury**.

UNEP has sponsored the development of solar loan programmes.

The solar loan programme sponsored by UN Environment helped finance solar power systems in India.

15.2. The Earth Summit

The Earth Summit, 1992: This was a direct consequence of the **Brundtland Commission's Report.** It was held in Rio de Janeiro. Conference held in Rio-De-Janerio, Brazil in 1992. **Former name: United Nations Conference on Environment and Development (UNCED)**

The Conference Give birth three important concept

1. Climate Change (UNFCCC):-

> ➢ **Kyoto Protocol**
> ➢ **Copenhagen accord**

2. Biodiversity (CBD:-Convention on Biological Diversity)

> ➢ **Aichi Targets**
> ➢ **Bio safety (Cartagena Biosafety protocol 2000)**
> ➢ **Nagoya Genetic Resources Protocol**

3. Sustainable Development

> ➢ **Agenda 21**
> ➢ **Rio-Summit**
> ➢ **Statement of forests**

Sustainable Development:

"Sustainable Development is development that meets the needs of the present, without compromising, the ability of future generations to meet their own needs".

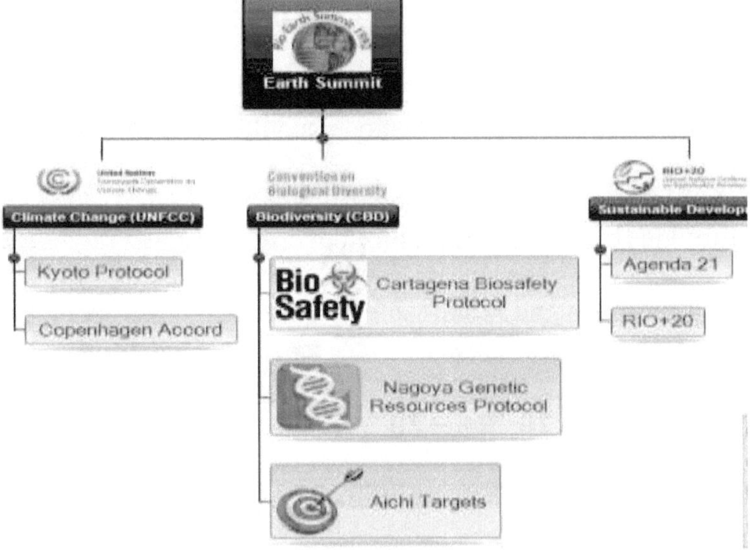

Fig.3.1. Earth Summit Timeline

Agenda 21

> ➢ Agenda 21 is a **non-binding,Voluntary** action plan of the **United Nations (UN)** related to **sustainable development**.
> ➢ It was an outcome of the **Earth Summit 1992**.

> The number 21 refers to an agenda for the 21st century.
> Its aim is achieving **global sustainable development**.
> Since 2015, **Sustainable Development Goals** are included in the Agenda 2030.

Rio Declaration

> 27 Principles and 3ʳᵈ generation rights
> Rio + 10(2002) Full implementation of Agenda 21
> Rio +20(2012) –Renew Political Commitment, implement gaps and address challenges
> 20 years of gap -1992 -2012
> Poverty Reduction
> Clean Energy
> Sustainable Development
> 7 Priority Areas
> Job, Energy, Cities, Food, water, Oceans and Disaster
> 49 page document -"Future We Want"

Statement of Forest principles
> This lead to the First global consensus on forest.
> The Developed country Nations should work to Green the world
> Develop Forest based on Soci0-Economic needs
> Provide financial resources for development
> 1994 working group on criteria and indicators for the conservations and sustainable management of temperatures and Boreal Forest started.

15.3. Rio+ 5, Rio+10, Rio+20,

Rio + 5(1997)

In 1997, the UN General Assembly held a special session to appraise the status of Agenda 21 (Rio +5).

> The Assembly recognized progress as "uneven" and identified key trends, including increasing globalization, widening inequalities in income, and continued deterioration of the global environment.

Rio+ 10(2002) or Earth Summit 2002

> **Rio+10 (2002) or Earth Summit 2002 or World Summit on Sustainable Development.**
> Took place in Johannesburg, South Africa in 2002.
> Rio+10 affirmed UN commitment to Agenda 21, alongside the Millennium Development Goals.
> Full implementation of Agenda 21.
> **Johannesburg Declaration**: committing the nations of the world to sustainable development.

Rio + 20 (2012)

> **Rio+20 (2012) or United Nations Conference on Sustainable Development.**
> Rio+20 was a 20-year follow-up to the Earth Summit 1992 and 10-year follow-up to the Earth Summit 2002.
> It is also known as Rio 2012 or Earth Summit 2012.
> Hosted by Brazil in Rio de Janeiro in 2012.
> It reaffirmed the commitment to **Agenda 21**.
> It was the third international conference on **sustainable development**.

Earth Summit 1992 (Rio de Janeiro) = UN Conference on Environment and Development (UNCED)
Earth Summit 2002 (Johannesburg) = World Summit on Sustainable Development (WSSD)
Earth Summit 2012 (Rio de Janeiro) = UN Conference on Sustainable Development (UNCSD)

PAGE, launched in 2013, is a direct response to the RIO+20 Declaration
The Fute We Want.Partnership for Action on Green Economy (PAGE)

- UNEP defined Green Economy "Economy Development with sustainable Development.A green economy is defined as low carbon resource efficient and socially inclusive.
- Rio+20 Declaration called upon the UN system and the international community to aid interested countries in

developing, adopting and implementing **green economy policies** and strategies.

- PAGE supports nations in reframing economic policies and practices around sustainability.
- PAGE seeks to assist countries in achieving **SDG (2030 Agenda),** especially SDG 8: **"Promote sustained, inclusive and sustainable economic growth, full and productive employment."**
- PAGE brings together the expertise of **five UN agencies – UNEP, ILO, UNIDO, UNDP** and **UNITAR.**
- **UNEP:** United Nation Environmental Programme
- **UNDP:** United Nation Development Program
- **ILO:** International Labour Organization
- **UNIDO:** UN Industrial Development Organization
- **UNITAR**: UN Institute for Training and Research.

15.4. Convention on Biological Diversity 1992

Convention is an International Agreement.

Convention on Biodiversity is the brainchild of United Nations Environment Programme (UNEP).

Headquarter is Montreal, Canada. It works under UNEP.

Biodiversity Conservation is a collective responsibility of all nations.

Convention on Biological Diversity (CBD) is a step towards conserving biological diversity or biodiversity with **the involvement of the entire world.**

The Convention on Biological Diversity (a multilateral treaty) was opened for signature at the **Earth Summit in Rio de Janeiro in 1992** and entered into effect in 1993.

The convention called upon all nations to take appropriate measures for conservation of biodiversity and **sustainable utilization** of its benefits.**Convention on Biodiversity CBD wants three aims**

1. Protecting Biodiversity   : COP meetings, Aichi Targets
2. Safe use of Biotechnology : Cartagena Biosafety Protocol

- **To Stop illegal use of Genetic Resources : Nagoya Genetic Resources Protocol**
- It is often seen as the key document regarding **Sustainable Development**.
- The Convention is **legally binding**; countries that join it ('Parties') are obliged to implement its provisions.
- 195 UN states and the European Union are parties to the convention.
- All UN member states, with the exception of the **United States**, have ratified the treaty.
- At the 2010 10th Conference of Parties (COP) to the Convention on Biological Diversity in October in Nagoya, Japan, the **Nagoya Protocol** was adopted.

15.5.Cartagena Biosafety/Cartagena Protocol 2000

Adopted in 2000,29[th] Jan,2022(Montreak,Canada0),Member-171.
COP 5 –Opened for signature 2000
Adopted in 2000 and rectified in 2003 and came into force in 2004.
The Cartagena protocol on Biosafety to the CBD is an international agreement

Aims

To ensure the safe handling, transport and use of **LMOs** –Living Modified Organisms by Biotechnology.
Establish Biosafety clearing House.
CBD covers the rapidly expanding field of **biotechnology** through its **Cartagena Protocol on Biosafety**
It addresses technology development and transfer, benefit-sharing and **Biosafety issues.**
The **Biosafety Protocol seeks to protect biological diversity** from the potential risks posed by living modified organisms resulting from modern biotechnology.

<table><tr><td>COP-10 Under CBD 2010
The Parties countries under convention on Biodiversity CBD meet at regular interval these meeting are called COP Conference of Parties.
10th such meeting was held at Aichi District of Nagoya,Japan 2010</td></tr></table>

This Cop-10 gave birth to two things
1.Aichi Targets for Biodiversity
2.Nagoya Protocol on Genetic Resources

15.6.Aichi Biodiversity Targets

- In the COP-Conference of Parties -10 the parties agreed that previous biodiversity protection targets are not achieved .So we need to do come up with new plans.
- **a.Short term by 2020 as " Strategic Plan Biodiversity 2011-2020.**
- **b. Long-term by 2050**
- This short termed is officially known as **"Strategic plan for Biodiversity 2011 -2020"**
- It is a ten year framework for action by all countries to save biodiversity.
- This short term plan targets **2010-2020 is called Aichi Targets.**

20 Targets in 5 sections (A to E)

Goal A– Address causes of Biodiversity loss

Goal B- Reduce direct pressure on Biodiversity and promote sustainable use

Goal C- Safeguards ecosystem species and genetic diversity

Goal D- Biodiversity benefits to all

Goal E- Participatory planning, capacity building

15.7.Nagoya Genetic Resources Protocol 2014

- Came in force in 2014
- It is an International agreement
- It is the **second Protocol to the CBD**; the first is the 2000 Cartagena Protocol on Biosafety.
- It is a 2010 supplementary agreement to the 1992 Convention on Biological Diversity (CBD).
- **The Nagoya Protocol Aim** is to sharing the benefit **arising from the utilization of genetic resources in a fair and equitable way.**

15.8.Climate Change: UNFCCC
United Nations Framework Convention on climate change

- ➢ International environmental treaty that came into existence under the aegis of UN.
- ➢ UNFCCC is negotiated at the **Earth Summit 1992.**
- ➢ Signed in **1992, New York** City.
- ➢ As of March 2019, UNFCCC has **197 parties.**
- ➢ **Role:** UNFCCC provides a framework for negotiating specific international treaties (called "protocols") that **aim to set binding limits on greenhouse gases.**
- ➢ Objective of UNFCCC: **Stabilize greenhouse gas concentrations** in the atmosphere at a level that would prevent dangerous consequences.
- ➢ Legal Effect: Treaty is considered **legally non-binding.**
- ➢ The treaty itself **sets no binding limits on greenhouse gas emissions for individual countries.**

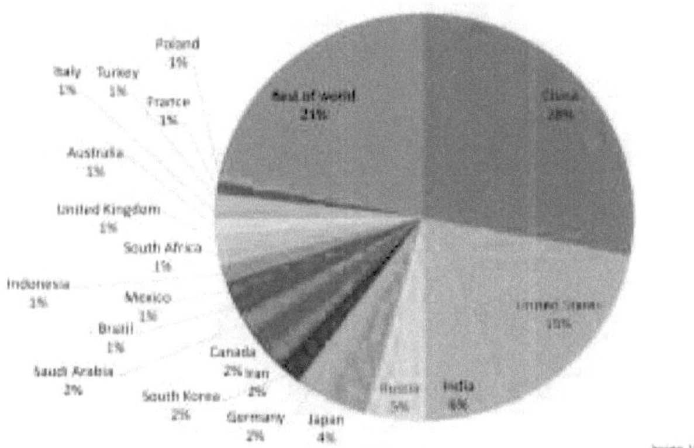

COP-UNFCCC

- ➢ The COP is the **decision-making body** of UNFCCC.
- ➢ All States that are Parties to the Convention are represented at the COP.
- ➢ They review the implementation of any legal instruments that the COP adopts.

- ➢ They promote the effective implementation of the Convention.
- ➢ The first COP meeting was held in **Berlin, Germany in March 1995**.
- ➢ The parties to the convention have met **annually** since 1995.
- ➢ In 1997, the **Kyoto Protocol (3ʳᵈ COP)** was concluded and established **legally binding obligations for developed countries to reduce their greenhouse gas emissions**.
- ➢ **COP 21 (2015) was held in Paris in 2015**.
- ➢ COP 22 (2016) was held at Marrakesh, Morocco.
- ➢ COP 23 (2017) was held at Bonn, Germany.
- ➢ **COP 24 (2018) was held at IFEMA,Madrid,Spain,2ⁿᵈ-13ᵗʰ Dec2019.**.

Climate Change Initiatives

1. First World Climate Conference   (1979)
2. COP-1 in Berlin 1995
3. Kyoto Protocol 1997
   Adopted -2005 in force
4. Copenhengen accord
   2009
5. Cancum 2010
6. Doha Amendment 2012
7. Lima Call for action 2014
8. Paris Agrement 2015
9. Marrakesh Agreement 2016
10. Bonn,Germany, Agreement 2017
11. Katowice Poland Agreement 2018: **Theme one world, One Sun, One Grid.**

•Rio +20 •SDGs targets, indicators

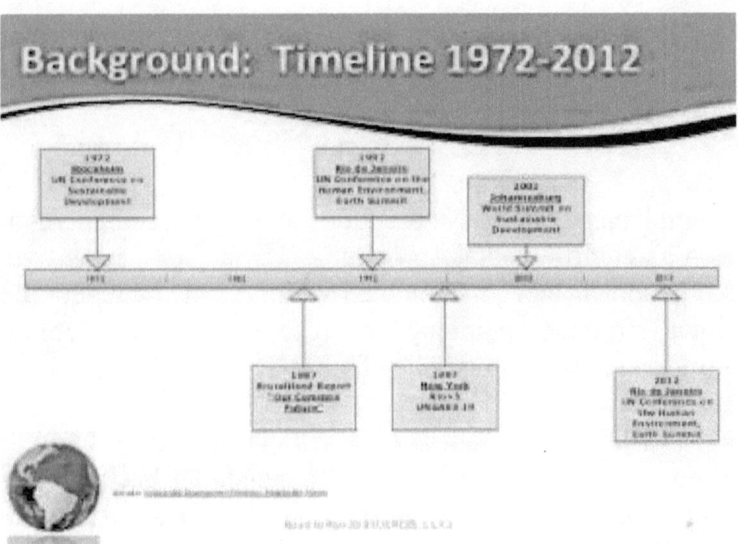

Fig.3.2: Timeline of International Convention 1972-2012

3.16. Concept and scope of environmental Management

What is environmental Management ?

Environmental management (EM) is a subject that combines science, policy, and socioeconomic applications. It primarily stresses on finding solution to practical problems that people face in cohabitation with nature, resource exploitation, and waste production. In a purely anthropocentric sense, environmental management is all about dealing with the fundamental issue of how to innovate technology to evolve continuously while limiting the degree to which this process alters natural environment. Thus, Environmental management is closely linked with issues regarding sustainable economic growth, ensuring fair and equitable distribution of resources, and conserving natural resources for future generations. Environmental management is a response to human actions considering the increasing seriousness and significance of today's disastrous human impact on natural ecosystems. It is comforting to know that with a smaller global population base and a less pervasive use of technology, the environment might be able to recuperate on its own from human misuse and abuse, but it is now widely recognized fact that in many cases positive intervention is necessary if the environment is to recover in view of the fact that people have bestowed more importance on economic growth than preservation of the natural ecosystems.

Definition

'Environmental management system refers to the management of an organization's environmental programs in a comprehensive, systematic, planned and documented manner. It includes the organizational structure, planning and resources for developing, implementing and maintaining policy for environmental protection'.
Some other definitions of EM
'The process of allocating natural and artificial resources so as to make optimum use of the environment in satisfying basis human needs, at the minimum, and more, if possible, on a sustainable basis'.**(Jolly,1978)**
Throughout the world, particularly in developing countries, there is an urgent need for the management of tool environment.In the first instance environment management must do three things
1. identify goal
2.Establish whether these can be met and
3.Develop and implement means to do what it deems possible.

Characteristic of Environmental Management.

1.Environmental management supports sustainable development
2.Environmental management demands the multi-disciplinary approach. It deals with a world affected by humans.
3.Environmental management has to integrate different development view points.
4.Environmental management seeks to integrate natural and social science
5.Environmental management can extend from short-term to long term and from local to global level.

Objectives of environmental management

Environmental management is an approach which integrates ecology, policy making, planning and social development. Its main objective are as follow:-
-to prevent and solve environmental problems,

-to establish limits
-To develop research institutions and monitoring systems.
-To warn threats and identify opportunities,
-to suggest measures for resources conservation.
-To develop a strategy for the improvement of quality.
-to suggest long-term and short -term policies for sustainable development.

Scope of environmental management
The scope of environmental management is a broad and comprehensive aspects of maintaining and improving environmental quality.
Awareness regarding environmental problems and their proper management began in 1970s through various people movement around many countries of the world.
the Green peace movement, the Chipko movement etc are some of them.The advancement in the field of science and technology helped to provide various tools and instruments supported by statistical data to properly solve environmental problems and help in its management.
The broader scopes of environmental management includes;
-to identify the environmental problem and to find its solution
-to restrict and regulate the exploitation & utilization of natural resources.
-To regenerate degraded environment and to renew natural resources(renewable)
-To control environmental pollution and gradation
-To reduce the impacts of extreme events & natural disaster
-To make optimum utilization of natural resources.
-To assess the impacts of proposed projects and activities on environment.
The scopes in the following areas need environmental management.
1.Population increase and health services.
2.Treatment of pollutants(air,water and solid)generated from various sources.
3.Pollution level in air,water and soil
4.Development of non-polluting renewable energy sources like wind,solarmbiomass,etc.
5.Solid waste utilization through recycling

6.Biodiversity conservation
7.environmental awareness in society.

Importance of EMS

An EMS addresses the environmental impact of an organization's activities and establishes goals and procedures that will improve the impact it has on the environment and human health.
1.Federal compliance-Clean Water Act, Clean Air, and The toxic substance control Act.
2.Public health
3.Emergency planes.

3.17. Solid Waste

Ever increasing population growth, urbanization and industrialization are contributing to the generation of waste from various sectors like agricultural, commercial, domestic, industrial, and institutional in massive quantities.

The term waste refers to the useless material generated from different sources such as household, public places, hospitals, commercial centre construction sites, industrial, etc.

Watse can be classified on the basis of physical state i.e., solid ,liquid and gaseous, and then within solid it is classified according to its origin i.e., domestic, industrial, commercial construction or institutional; according to its contents i.e., organic material, glass, metal, plastic paper etc.; or according to hazard potential i.e., toxic, non-toxic, flammable, radioactive ,infectious etc.

3.18. Classification of Solid waste

1. Domestic waste
2. Municipal Solid waste
3.Industrial Waste
4.Agricultural waste
5.Institutional wastes
6.Hazardous waste
7.Infectious waste : Biomedical waste
9.E-Waste

Domestic waste:
These wastes are generated from household, preparation and weeping. The common ingredients are old paper, cloth, bottles, plastics, crockery waste, vegetables waste etc.

Municipal Solid Waste(MSW)
Municipal Solid waste is also called as trash or garbage. In general, domestic waste and municipal solid waste are used as synonyms. Actually, in term Municipal Solid Waste is used to describe most of the non-hazardous solid waste from a town or city or village.
The main sources of MSW include private homes, commercial establishments and institutions, as well as industrial facilities. Nevertheless, municipal solid waste does not include wastes from industrial processes, construction and demolition debris, sewage sludge, mining waste or agricultural waste. Municipal Solid waste contains a wide variety of materials such as food waste like meat and vegetable materials, eggshells leftover food. Etc., which is tetrapack, carboard boxes, newspaper, aluminium foil glass bottles, meat items ,wood pieces etc., which is classified as dry garbage.
The different types of municipal solid wastes or domestic waste generated and the time taken for them to degenerate is illustrated in the table given below:

Types of Domestic waste	Time taken to degeneration (Appx)
Organic Kitchen waste vegetables, fruits	1 to 14 Days
Paper, cardboard paper	15-30 Days
cotton clothes	2-5 months
Woolen clothes	1 year
Metal cans,tin,aluminium	100-500 years
Plastics	1 million years

Industrial Wastes
It includes the wastes of domestic and commercial nature generated from the office, canteen, staff quarters of the small cottage industries operating in the municipalities and industrial estates.

Agricultural waste

These wastes generally consist of hay, animal dung, the remains of pesticides, herbicides and weedicides also contributes significantly to agricultural waste.

Institutional wastes

Schools, colleges, universities. Research institutes, development organisation, community halls and religious places generate waste like paper, rejected office stationery, etc.

Hazardous waste

Hazardous wastes refer to materials that are danger or potentially harmful to human health or the environment. This can include chemicals, industrial by products, and other substance that are reactive, corrosive, toxic, flammable.

Infectious waste / Biomedical waste

Waste generated from hospitals, nursing homes, clinic. The wastes are disposable syringes, used surgical dressing, expired drugs, etc, which are highly contaminated and are not taken, this will creates lots of severe infectious diseases.

E-Waste

Electronic wastes or e-waste is defined as unwanted and non-working electronic products which are nearing or at the end of its useful life.

This includes used and broken electronics which are mean for reuse, resale, recover, recycling, or disposal as well as reusables which are working and repairable electronics and secondary scraps such as steel, copper, plastics etc.

3.19. Solid Waste Management

The activities involved with the management of solid wastes from the point generation to final disposal have been grouped into six functional element:

1. Waste generation
2. On-site handling, storage and processing
3. Colelction
4. Transfer and transport
5. Processing and recovery
6. Disposal

Description of the Functional elements of a solid waste management system.

Functional Elements	Description
Waste generation	Those activities in which materials are identified as no longer being of value and are either throw away or gathered for disposal
On site handling storaging and processing	Those activities associated with the handling, storage, and process of solid waste at or near the point of generation.
Collection	Those activities associated with the gathering of solid wastes and the hauling or waste after collection to the location where the collection vehicle is emptied.
Transfer and Transport	Those activities associated with(1) the transfer to waste from the smaller collection vehicle to the larger transport equipment and (2) the subsequent transport of the wastes to the disposal site
Processing and recovery	Those techniques, cover equipment and facilities used both to improve the efficiency of the other functional elements and to recover materials or energy from solid wastes.
Disposal	Those activities associated with ultimate disposal of solid waste, including those waste collected and transported directly to landfill site.

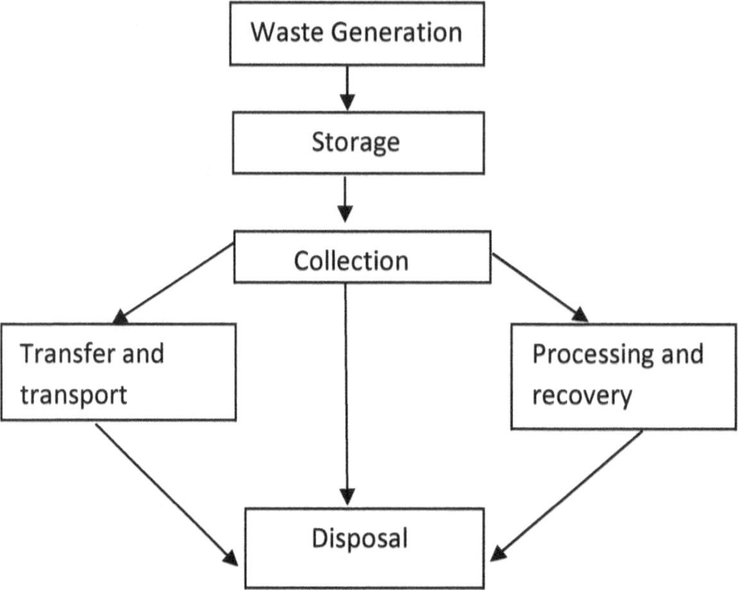

Fig.4.1 . Solid waste Management

Solid Waste Management:-

The activities involved with the management of solid wastes from the point generation to final disposal have been grouped into six functional elements:

Solid waste management can be classified into following six key components

    1. Waste Generation

    2. Storage

    3. Collection

    4. Transfer and transport

    5. Treatment/ processing and recovery

    6. Disposal

1. Waste generation:-

The quantity and characteristics of solid waste varying from place to place Factors that affect the generation of waste are population, social behaviour, climate, industrial production, changing life style and the market for waste materials.

2. Storage:-
Those activities associated with the handling, storage and process of solid waste at or near the point of generation.
The handing, processing of solid waste at sources before there collected is the second of the six functional elements in solid waste management system.
The factors that must be considered in theOnsite storage of solid waste includes.

1. Type of container to be used.
2. The container location.
3. Public health and aesthetics.
4. Collection methods to be used.

3. Collection
Those activities associated with the gathering of solid wastes and hauling of wastes after collection to the location where the collection vehicles is emptied.
The waste are separated and collected at one place and after that they are transported for the further process.
It can do by four parts

1. The types of collection services
2. The types of collection systems
3. An analysis of collection systems.
4.The general methodology involved in setting up collection routes.

4.Transfer and Transport
- **Those activities are carried out as Transfer of waste from the smaller collection vehicle to the larger Transport equipment and**
- **The subsequent transport of waste, usually over long distance, to the disposal site.**
- Transfer and transport operation become a necessity when haul distances to available disposal site or processing center increase to the point that direct hauling is no longer economical feasible.

> Motor vehicles, railroads, and ocean going vessels are the principal means now used to transport solid wastes. Pneumatic and hydraulic system has also been used. But these days railroad transport and water transport is no longer practices

Motor Vehicle Transport

Motor Vehicles used to transport solid wastes on highways should satisfy the following requirements

    1.The vehicles must transport wastes at minimum costs

    2.Wastes must be covered during the haul operation

    3. Vehicles capacity must be such that allowable weight limits not exceeded.

    4. Vehicle must be designed for highway traffic

    5. Methods used for unloading must be simple and dependable

5. Processing and Recovery:-

Those techniques, equipments and facilities passed for both to improve the efficiency of the other functional element and to recover usable material, conversion products, or energy from solid waste.

6.Disposal:-

Disposal on or in the earth mantle is, at present, the only viable method is land filling. Land filling is method of disposal used most commonly for municipal waste; land filling and deep-well injection have been used for industrial waste. Although incineration is often considered a disposal method, it is, in reality, a processing method.

There is various method of disposal as follow:-

    1. Open Dumping
    2. Landfills
    3. Sanitary landfills
    4. Ocean dumping
    5. Incineration
    6. Vermicomposting/Vermiculture
    7. Biomethanation
    8. Pyrolysis

3.19. Waste to wealth technologies

Waste to wealth refers to the process of converting waste materials into valuable resources, thereby creating economic, environmental, and social benefits.

Waste to wealth initiatives are increasingly important in achieving sustainability goals and fostering a circular economy where resources are used efficiently and waste is minimized.

Modern Waste to wealth Technologies

Here are Some waste to wealth technologies.

1.Biological Processes:

i.Composting: Decomposing organic waste into nutrient-rich compost used in agriculture.

Composting is the aerobic and thermophilic decomposition of organic matter present in the refuse by microorganisms, primarily bacteria and fungi.This organic matter is transformed into stable humus like substance during this process. The reactions taking place during composting generate heat and hence the compost temperature rises during the process. Depending upon the composition and nature of the waste, the volume is reduced by about 30% to 60 %.

ii.Anaerobic Digestion: Breaking down organic waste in the absence of oxygen to produce biogas (methane and carbon dioxide) and digestate (used as fertilizer).

2.Mechanical and Physical Processes:

i.Recycling: Sorting and processing materials like plastics, paper, glass, and metals for reuse in manufacturing.

Recycling is one of the fundamental parts of the waste management plant. Although it alone cannot solve a community's municipal SWM problem, it can divert a significant portion of waste stream from disposal in landfill and combustion facilities.

ii.Pyrolysis: Thermal decomposition of organic materials in the absence of oxygen to produce bio-oil, biochar, and syngas.

In this process the combustible constituents of the solid waste are heated in a special retort like chamber know as a pyrolysis reactor at 600-1000'c in a low oxygen or an oxygen free environment. This is an endothermic process and thus differs from the conventional incinerations.

Pyrolysis of the solid waste yield the following components:

1. Tar or oil phase containing methanol, acetone, acetic acid ,etc.
2. Gaseous phase containing H_2,CH_2,CO,CO_2,etc.

3.Solid phase containing pure carbon char and inert materials like glass, rock metal etc.

Advantage: Volume reduction by about 90%,Absence of pollution problems.

Gasification: Converting carbonaceous materials into synthesis gas (syngas), which can be used as a fuel.

3.Chemical Processes:

Plasma Arc Gasification: Using plasma to break down waste materials at high temperatures, converting them into syngas and slag.

It is an advanced waste treatment technology that uses extremely high temperatures generated by a plasma torch to convert waste materials into synthetic gas(syngas) and solid residue(slag)

Hydrothermal Treatment: Treating organic waste with water at elevated temperatures and pressures to break down complex molecules into simpler compounds.

4.Technologies for Specific Waste Types:

E-Waste Recycling: Dismantling and recycling electronic waste to recover valuable metals like gold, silver, copper, and rare earth elements.

Construction and Demolition Waste Recycling: Separating and processing materials like concrete, wood, and metals for reuse in construction.

5.Energy Recovery:

Waste-to-Energy (WtE): Burning solid waste to generate electricity or heat, reducing the volume of waste and producing energy.

6.Emerging Technologies:

Nanotechnology: Using nanoparticles for efficient water purification and environmental remediation.

Blockchain: Tracking waste streams and ensuring transparency and accountability in waste management.

7.Integration and Scaling:

Circular Economy Models: Promoting closed-loop systems where waste is minimized, and materials are continually reused and recycled.

Circular economy models are designed to minimized waste, maximize resource efficiency, and foster sustainable economy growth

Smart Waste Management: Utilizing IoT (Internet of Things) and AI (Artificial Intelligence) for real-time monitoring and optimization of waste processes.

These technologies play a crucial role in addressing global waste challenges, promoting sustainability, and creating economic opportunities through resource recovery and reuse.

UNIT 4
ENVIRONMENTAL HAZARDS

4.1.Hazard

Anything that has the potential to cause harm, injuries, damage to property and environment. Hazard is a dangerous event, natural or human induced that could cause injury, loss of life or damage to property, livelihood or environment. For Example: Natural Hazards: Flood, Landslide, drought, tsunami, volcanic eruption. Men-Made Hazard: dam failure, leakage of toxic waste, war, road accident, rail, industrial ,terror attacks.

4.2.Risk:

The probability of any injury or loss occurring from the hazards.
A risk is the combination of the probability of the hazardous event occurring and the consequences of the events

Risk Assessment

It is a systematic investigation and analysis of potential risk, combined with the assignment of severities of probabilities and consequences.

The main objective of risk assessment is for the prevention of accidents and ill-health

Steps of Risk Assessment
There are five steps to Risk Assemment
1.Identifying the hazards
2.Identifying the people who might be harmed and how
3.Evaluate the risk and implement control measures.
4.Record the significant findings and implement them

5.Review and update the risk assessment: Regularly review and update the Risk assessment to ensure effectiveness and account for any changes in the work environment or processes.

4.3.Vulnerability: Vulnerability is defined as "the extent to which a community, structure, service, or geographic area is like to be damaged or disrupted by the impact of particular hazards, on account of their nature, construction and proximity of hazardous terrain or a disaster prone area.

Vulnerability refers to a state of being exposed or susceptible to harm, risk, or negative impacts. It is a concept that can be applied to certain communities, individuals or area or societies.

It can be arise from various factors like social, economic, environmental or personal circumstances.

4.4.Types of vulnerability

1.Physical Vulnerability

Physical Vulnerability related to the physical location of people their proximity to the hazards zone and standards of safety maintenance to counter the effects.

Example: People are only vulnerable to a floods because they live in a flood prone area.

2.Socio-Economic Vulnerability

Disparate capacity of people, community are exposed disaster, which explains differential vulnerability losses.

4.5.Disaster

The word disaster has been taken from the French word **desastre** (French des means "bad" and aster means a star, destiny).

Earlier in the past,the disasters were considered as punishment given by nature for interfering with it.

According to WHO.An extraordinary event of limited duration which causes serious disruption of economy of the country.

A Disaster is the serious disruption or destruction or loss of material or environment which the affected community is usable to cope up the loss using its own resources.
It impact and affect the way in which we live.

Disaster can also be defined as an extreme event either natural or man-caused which exceeds the toleration limits, makes adjustment difficult and results into catastrophic loss of life and property.

Effect of Disaster:
Disasters differ according to their nature, magnitude of the destruction and also in terms of their severity, disruptive potential and duration. The effects of disaster depend upon the types of disaster.
-Natural disaster like earthquakes, flood, storm, landslides, etc., have immediate effect-they destroy houses, roads, physical and social infrastructure, production facilities and crops.
-Continuing disasters (like drought, crop failure has slow effect-they create compound long standing problems like deforestation, desertification, soil erosion and create pressure on urban centres.
-Man-made disasters lead to population explosion, environmental degradation and effect infrastructure as well as economic actives.
Disaster disrupts physical as well as economic.

4.6.Types of Disaster
    1. Man-Made Disaster:
    2. Natural Disaster
6.1.Natural Disaster
Disaster which are caused by violent forces of nature suddenly and are beyond the control of humans are called **natural disasters.**
Main Example of natural disaster are given below-
Major Disaster: Floods, Earthquakes, cyclones landslides, volcanic eruptions, Tsunamis, Droughts etc.
Minor Disaster: Cold wave,Thunderstorms,Heat wave, mud slides.

6.1.a.Floods

Flood is natural as well as manmade disaster which affects human habitation over large areas causing loss of lives and property.

It is an overflow of a large amount of water beyond its normal limits, especially over dry land. It is result of long period of heavy rainfall from overflowing rivers, sudden cloud burst, from sudden melting of snow, cyclone, dam collapse etc.

Flood cause great distress as they damage crops, property and also life. Home are destroyed making people homeless. It also erodes soil.

Flood awareness: Always listen to media, radio, TV for warning and prediction. Move to safe places, away from flood prone areas.

6.1.b.Earthquakes

Earthquakes are natural phenomena. They are the most sudden of all disasters, and come without any warning. Thus, they are not predictable to preventable.

Most earthquakes are minor tremors. Large earthquakes usually begin with minor tremors but rapidly take the form of one or more violent shocks, and end in vibrations of gradually diminishing force called aftershocks.

Most of the damage is caused not by the earthquake but by the buildings that we live in, especially in urban or semi-urban areas with concrete structure.

Earthquakes are measured with a seismometer, device which also Records is known as a seismograph. The moment the magnitude (or the related and mostly obsolete Richter magnitude) of an earthquake is conventionally reported, with magnitude 3 or lower earthquakes being mostly imperceptible and magnitude 7 causing serious damage over large areas. Intensity of shaking is measured on the modified Mercalli scale.

Caused of Earthquakes

1.Crustal Instability: The tectonic forces are generally the main cause of earthquakes. They lead to sudden movements of the crustal blocks. Thus, a majority of earthquakes are associated with areas of crustal instability and each earthquakes are called" Tectonic Earthquakes' e.g. the 2015 earthquakes in Nepal.

2.Volcanic Eruptions: Volcanic eruptions also caused many earthquakes. They accompany most of the explosive eruptions. Such earthquakes are said to be of "Volcanic Origin'

Effect of Earthquakes:

1.Changes in the earth's crust may lead to a number of indirect effects such as landslides, avalanches, tsunamis even as in 2004 Indian Ocean and blocking of course of rivers and subsequent flooding when the blockage is removed by accumulated water.

2.Liquification of the soil and landslides occur due to earthquakes.

3.It may damage large dams, power installations and even nuclear power plants.

6.1.c.Cyclones

The words cyclone is derived from the Greek word" Cyclos' meaning coil of a snake.

Mr.Paddington of the Calcutta(Now Kolkata)port during the middle of the last century named these weather systems as **cyclone** because of spiral shape of cloud bonds.

Cyclones are violent storms,often of vast extent;these are associated with turbulent weather condition with high velocity winds,cloudiness and rainfall.

It is a sweirling atmosphere disturbance, 300 km per hour blowing in a clockwise direction in the Northern hemisphere, and anti-clock-wise direction in the southern hemisphere,by pouring rain, and generating enormous waves in the ocean.

Most damages from cyclones are caused by the strong winds, torrential rains and high storm tides. During intense cyclone people are advised to stay alert and stay awake, to stay inside the homes, be alert for any sudden increase or decrease in water flow.

6.1.d.Landslide

A landslide is the movement of rock, debris or earth down a slope. They result from the failure of the materials which make up the hill slope and are driven force of gravity. It may be caused by an earthquake but it generally the result of rain soaking the ground. It is very common in mountainous regions along eroding rivers and coastline

6.2.Man-made Disaster

Man-Made Disaster:

Man-Made Disaster are caused by Human activities such as nuclear explosion, chemical and biological weapons, industrial pollution, war, riots, accidents etc.

Some serious destruction caused by humans, which affects the human beings and socio-economic conditions of that area,

For example; Use of Atom Bomb in 1945, Bhopal Ga Tragedy 1984, Serial Blasts in Mumbai in 2008, COVID19 Etc.

4.7.Mitigation and Mitigation Strategies

Any measures taken to minimize the impact of a disaster or potential disaster.

Mitigation can be taken place before, during or after a disaster, but the term is most often used to refer to action taken against potential disasters,

Disaster management/Disaster Mitigation is also called emergency management.

It is the discipline of dealing with and avoiding risks. In general, it is the continuous process by which all individuals., groups and communities manage hazards in an effort to avoid or minimize the impact of the disasters resulting from the hazards.

It is almost impossible to fully control the damage caused by the disaster, but it is possible to minimize to some extent by following ways:

Disaster can be minimize to some extent by following ways:-
By early warning given by Metrological Department through radio and TV, using developed contemporary forecasting and early warning systems.
By spreading awareness about disasters and tips to handle them.
Every citizen must cooperate with the rescue teams

Mitigation Strategy:
Mitigation strategies are actions and measures designed to reduce or eliminate the impact of potential hazards and disasters before they occur. The goal of mitigation is to minimize and reduce the damage cause, protect lives and property, and improve overall resilience to future events.

List of main elements of effective mitigation strategy
There are four Important phase of Disaster Management/Mitigation.
1.Preparedness:
2.Response and relief
3.Recovery/Rehabitation and reconstruction
4.Mitigation/Prevention.

Four Phases of Emergency Management

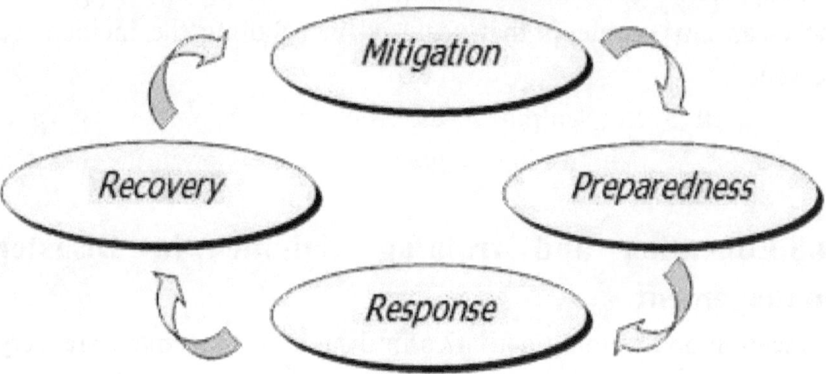

Preparedness

First, prepare to protect yourself, others and items of great importance in the event an emergency/disaster occurs. It involves measures that enable Government, communities and individuals to respond rapidly to disaster situation and cope with them effectively

Response and relief

When there is an actual occurrence, administer first aid or get medical attention for victims if necessary. Attend to other emergency procedures that must take place in order to lessen the impact.

Immediate measure is taken up in anticipation of disasters to ensure that the effects are minimized. These are normally carried out simultaneously after a disaster.

Recovery/Rehabitation and reconstruction

After things are under control, begin the clean up or repair any damage and if necessary, call in professional restoration services.

Government, NGOs which would help affected community to come back normally.

Mitigation/Prevention

Finally, ask how did this disaster, accident or emergency happen and how can any problems that occurred in handling the incident be lessened.

Any action taken to minimize the extent of a disaster is known as mitigation. Mitigation can take place before, after or during disaster.

4.8. Education and training activities in Disaster management

Education and training activities in disaster management are very important for ensuring effective preparedness, response, and recovery for disaster management. They consisting a wide range of activities aimed at improving knowledge, skills, and capabilities related to disaster management.

Following are the important Key components to be consider:
1.Public Awareness Campaigns: Educating the school children, general public about disaster risks, safety measures, and preparedness actions. This includes distributing information through various media and community events.

2.Emergency Response Drills: Conducting simulated exercises to practice response procedures, test communication systems, and improve coordination among emergency services and community members.

3.Training Programs for First Responders: Providing specialized training for firefighters, police, medical personnel, and other first responders on handling emergencies, using equipment, and performing life-saving techniques.

4.Organising Community level Training: Offering different awareness program and workshops and courses for community members on topics such as first aid, emergency planning, and self-defense during disasters management in the community level.

5.Technical Training for Specialists: Training for professionals involved in disaster management, such as risk analysts, planners, and engineers, on advanced topics like hazard assessment, risk reduction strategies, and disaster recovery.

6.Capacity Building for Organizations: Strengthening the skills and knowledge of organizations involved in disaster management, including non-profits, governmental agencies, and private sector partners.

7.Educational Programs in Schools: Integrating disaster preparedness and safety education into school curriculums to teach students about risks and how to act in emergencies.

8.Simulations and Tabletop Exercises: Running simulations and discussion-based exercises to explore disaster scenarios, improve decision-making, and refine

By investing in these education and training activities, communities and organizations can enhance their readiness, response capabilities, and overall resilience to disasters.

4.9.Planning for Rescue and Relief works During Disaster Management

Proper planning for rescue and relief work during disaster management involves several key steps to ensure an effective and coordinated response.

Some essential components required for rescue and relief during disaster management are as follows

1.Risk Assessment and Resource Mapping: Identify the types of disasters that may occur and assess the resources available, such as personnel, equipment, and supplies. Map out areas of high risk and critical infrastructure to prioritize response efforts needs to be taken.

2.Emergency Plans and Response: One need to Develop a detailed plans outlining procedure for rescue and relief operations. This includes establishing command structures, communication protocols, and roles and responsibilities for different teams and agencies, different NGOs, Govt administration.

3.Proper Coordination Mechanisms: Create systems for coordinating between various stakeholders, including government agencies, non-governmental organizations (NGOs), and community groups. Designate a central coordination hub for managing information and resources.

4.Training and Exercises: Conduct regular training for rescue and relief teams, including simulations and drills. This helps ensure that personnel are familiar with procedures and can operate effectively under pressure.

5.Resource Management: Plan for the acquisition, storage, and distribution of essential resources, such as medical supplies, food, water, and shelter materials. Establish logistics networks to manage the flow of these resources to affected areas.

6.Communication Systems: Implement robust communication systems to ensure timely and accurate information exchange. This includes setting up emergency communication channels and backup systems in case of failures.

7.Public Information and Support: Develop strategies for providing accurate information to the public and managing media relations. Offer support services such as mental health counselling and legal aid to disaster survivors.

8.Post-Disaster Evaluation: After a disaster, conduct assessments to evaluate the effectiveness of rescue and relief efforts. Gather feedback from responders and affected individuals to identify lessons learned and improve future plans.

9.Community Engagement: Involve local communities in planning and preparedness activities. Ensure that community members are aware of how they can contribute and what to expect during a disaster.

By incorporating with the following key elements into disaster management planning, organizations and communities can enhance their readiness for rescue and relief operations, leading to more effective and timely assistance during emergencies.

4.10.Disaster management during earthquakes

Earthquakes give no warning at all. Sometimes, a loud rumbling sound might signal its arrival a few second ahead of time. Those few seconds could give you a chance to move to a safer location. Here are some few tips for keeping safe during a quake:

-Go under a table or other sturdy furniture's; kneel, sit, or stay close to the floor.

-If no sturdy cover is nearby, kneel or sit close to the floor next to a structurally sound interior wall.

-Move away from windows, mirrors, bookcases, and other unsecured heavy objects.

-If you are in bed, stay there and cover yourself with pillows and blankets.

-Never use the lift.

-If outdoor, move into a open, away from buildings, streetlights and utility wires. Once, it is open, stay there until the shaking stops.

-After the first tremor, be prepared for aftershocks. Though less intense, aftershocks cause additional damages and may bring down weakened structures. Aftershocks can occur in the first hours, days, weeks, or even month after the quake and maybe more intense sometimes.

-Listen to a mobile radio, Tv, for the latest emergency information.

4.11.Disaster management during landslide

-Stay alert and awake. Many debris-flow fatalities occur when people are sleeping. Listen to mobile radio or Television for warnings of intense rainfall.

-Listen for any unusual sounds that might indicate moving debris, such as trees cracking or boulders knocking together.

-If you are near a stream or channel, be alert for any sudden increase or decrease in water flow and for a change from clear to muddy water. Such changes may indicate landslide actively upstream.

-Be especially alert when driving, embankments along roadsides are particularly susceptible to landslide. Watch the road for collapsed pavement, mud, fallen rocks, and other indications of possible debris flows.

What response you will act if you suspect imminent landslide danger?

-Contact your local fire, police or public works department.Local officials are the best persons able to assess potential danger.

-inform affected neighbors.Your,neighbors may not be aware of potential hazrads.Advising them of a potential threat may help save lives.Help neighbors who may need assistance to evacuate.

-Evacuate, getting out of the path of a landslide or debris flow is your best protection.

Community Education:

-In an area prone to landslide, publish a special newspaper section with emergency information on landslides and debris flows.

-Report on what city, town Governments are doing to reduce the possibility of landslides.

-work with local emergency services to prepare special reports for people with mobility impairments on what to do if evacuation is ordered.

-Support your local government in efforts to develop and enforce land-use and building ordinances that regulate construction in areas susceptible to landslides and debris flows. Buildings should be located away from steep slopes, streams and rivers intermittent-stream channels, and the mouths of mountain channels.

What to do after the Landslide?

Stay away from the slide area. There may be danger of additional slides.

-check for injured and trapped persons near the slide, without entering the direct slide area. Direct rescuers to their locations.

-Listen to the media radio, Televisions for the latest emergency information.

-Watch for flooding, which may occur after a landslide or debris flow

-Replant damaged ground as soon as possible since erosion caused by loss of ground cover can lead to flash flooding.

Before a Landslide

Develop a family Disaster Plan. Develop landslide-specific planning.

Learn about landslide risk in your locality, contact local official, state geological survey or departments of natural resources and university department of geology.

4.12.Disaster management during floods

Mitigation measures

-Build dwelling units at least 250 metres away from the coast or river banks

-Avoid inhabitation on the slopes on river sides and sides of gorges.

-Construct the house with a plinth level higher than the previous flood level.

-Construct house a stilts or columns with lower ten feet higher without walls to allow free flow of water. The columns should be circular and dup rooted.

Before floods.

-All your family members should know the safe route to nearest shelter/raised concrete building.

-Have an emergency kit on hand which includes a portable radio torch and dry food, drinking water and clothes, water proof bags and bamboo stick (to protect from snake), salt and sugar etc.

-Have handy a First Aid Kits, manual and strong ropes for trying things.

-When you hear a flood warning, prepare to take bullock carts, other agricultural equipments, and domestic animals to safer places or to higher locations.

During floods

-Drink boiled water.

-Use raw tea, rice-water, tender coconut-water, etc. during diarrhoea contact your doctor for ORS and treatment.

-Do not let children remain with empty stomach.

-Use bleaching powder and lime to disinfect the surroundings.

-Help the officials/volunteers distributing relief materials.

If you need to evacuate:

Pack clothing, essential medications, valuables personal papers, etc in waterproof bags, to be taken with your emergency kit.

-Raise furniture, clothing and valuable onto beds, tables and to the top of the roof.

-Do not get into water of unknow depth and current.

www.ingramcontent.com/pod-product-compliance
Lightning Source LLC
Chambersburg PA
CBHW021549150726
47990CB00006B/2456